Collecting
AMERICAN COUNTRY

Collecting
AMERICAN COUNTRY

HOW TO SELECT, MAINTAIN, AND DISPLAY COUNTRY PIECES

BY MARY ELLISOR EMMERLING

PHOTOGRAPHS BY CHRIS MEAD
DESIGN BY RICHARD TRASK
TEXT BY CAROL COOPER GAREY

Clarkson N. Potter, Inc./Publishers   NEW YORK

DISTRIBUTED BY CROWN PUBLISHERS, INC.

To
Samantha and Jonathan, with love forever
My mother and father, for always being there
Chris, my best friend,
for his encouragement and support and his love

Published by Clarkson N. Potter, Inc., One Park Avenue,
New York, New York, 10016, and simultaneously in
Canada by General Publishing Company Limited
Manufactured in Japan

Library of Congress Cataloging in Publication Data
Emmerling, Mary Ellisor.
    Collecting American country.

    Bibliography: p.
    Includes index.
    1. Americana—Collectors and collecting. 2. Folk
art—United States—Collectors and collecting.
I. Mead, Chris.   II. Garey, Carol Cooper.   III. Title.
NK805.E45   1983   745.1'0973'075   83-2207
ISBN: 0-517-54957-3
10 9 8 7 6 5 4 3 2 1
First Edition

Acknowledgments

There could be no better opening to *Collecting American Country* than an "old friends" hooked rug. This book is for *you*—all of you who sent me your thoughts after reading *American Country,* wrote thank yous, invited me to see your country homes and collections. Your enthusiasm and your observations made me want to set out cross-country again in pursuit of another book.

Collecting American Country is for you and some very special people I want to thank personally. I am particularly grateful:

to Samantha and Jonathan Emmerling, who have inherited my love for country, antiquing, and traveling, and who make each new discovery a family holiday;

to Chris Mead for the time and effort he put into photographing and caring for the best picture. It is his eye for beauty and skill at photography that make this book so special. To him, always, I give my thanks and love;

to my agents Gayle Benderoff and Deborah Geltman, who are always there on the rough country roads and who have my eternal gratitude for that first phone call. My greetings to Laura Renee, who logged some miles along the way;

to Richard Trask, who came up with beautiful and ingenious ideas for the design of this book, to his daughter Kimberly, and to his wife, Jean, who was always there with moral support, a Pepsi, and never a complaint;

to Bernard Barenholtz, who has always been an inspiration to me, for offering a wealth of information and help on this book;

to Carol Cooper Garey, for her research and ability to turn a phrase;

to Jody Thompson, who seemed to know the solution to every problem and just kept on going, for her dedication, pursuit of information, interviews, and endless supply of humor;

to the staff of the American Country store, which opened because everyone seemed to want the American Country rabbit and good country accessories. My thanks to Jody Greif, Liza Rand, Susan Sawyer, and our Mrs. Brooks, and special gratitude to Margaret Degan Donohue for her work on the directories;

to all of you across the country whose collections or thoughts appear in this book, including Kathy Schoemer, who lent us the "old friends" hooked rug from her Country Collections; to Dottie and Manny Affler, Felipe Archuleta, Way Bandy, Charlotte and L. C. Beckerdite, Lester Breininger, Byron Bruffee, Mary Randolf Carter, Margaret Cavigga, Milton Chapin, Robert Congdon, Bill Corson, Burlon Craig, Susan and George Delagrange, Esprit De Corp and Doug Tomkins, Forest Fenn, Ed and Doris Gamson, Michael Gardine, Alexander and Susan Girard, Pat and Jim Godman, Emery Goff and Bill Carhart of the Old Barn Annex, Diane and Stan Gove, Barbara Gray, Gwen and Ron Griffin, Jane and George Harold, June Harrison, Sherman Hensal, Ian Ingersoll, Jerry Jeanmard, Barbara and Fred Johnson, Barbara and Norman Kaufman, Mary Kaufman, Barbara and Bob Kelley, Don Kelly and Warren Fitzsimmons, John and Kathy Killip, Bob Kinnaman and Brian Ramaekers, Rod Kiracofe and Michael Kile, Delores and Lowell Klaber, Joel and Kate Kopp, Charlene Kress, Horst and Hannelis Kuntze, Morgan and Gerri MacWhinnie, Paul Madden, Holly and Stephen Meier, Bettie and Seymour Mintz, Jim and Betty Murray, Edwa Osborn, Bill and Ruth Pierce, Tom and Carolyn Porter, Pat Ranallo, Jack and Alexandra Reynolds, Sally and Pete Riffle, Joe Ruggiero, Jerry Smith, Dr. George Ross Starr, Jr., Doris and Patricia Stauble, Marjorie Staufer, Barbara and Dan Strawser, Dick and Sue Studebaker, Bobbie Taylor, Nancy and Charlie Thomas, Marj Van Dusen and Pat Schuman, Donna and Paul Wagner, Beth Weisman, and alphabetically last, but in every other way first, Molly Wolford;

to my whole family, and especially my brother Terry, who has always been there for me and I know always will be, and to Steve and Nancy; to Juanita Jones, who remains faithful and loving with my children and with me; to Peter Frugone, who keeps me moving and living in the country style; and to my friends, who offer help, understanding, and unending support: Katrin Tolleson, Beverly Jacomini, Mibs Bird, Mary Higgins, Dick and Libby Kramer, Holly Meier, Peri Wolfman, and Barbara Brooks.

To everyone at Clarkson N. Potter, Inc., who has become my second family and particularly to Nancy Novogrod, my editor, whose new arrivals—this time Caroline—always seem to be on the same schedule as my books, and who tirelessly and unfailingly provides concepts, direction, and comments; to Nat Wartels, Chairman of Crown and Clarkson N. Potter, who continues to believe in American Country; Michael Fragnito, who steps in with a firm hold on schedules and temperaments; Carol Southern, Editorial Director; Kathy Powell, a master of organization, who provides suggestions and support; Lynne Arany, who oversees layouts with diligence and care; Gael Dillon, who helped; Ellen Tarlow and David Bauer, for their assistance; Ann Cahn for her careful evaluation; Laurie Stark and Teresa Nicholas for feats of production; Michelle Sidrane, Phyllis Fleiss, and Jo Fagan in subsidiary rights; Nancy Kahan and Susan Eilertsen in publicity; Gail Shanks in sales; and always to Jane West, who was one of the very first to know that country was really America.

Happy Country!

Mary Ellisor Emmerling
February 1983

Contents

Introduction

If your pulse quickens at the sight of a quizzical old Teddy bear, a timeworn weather vane, a walking stick smoothed by anonymous hands, you possess the sensibility of a collector. And if one discovery whets your appetite for another, you know the seductive powers that collecting holds.

Perhaps it's what Willa Cather called "that irregular and intimate quality of things made by the human hand" that lures collectors to objects from America's past. Or maybe it's the simplicity of rural crafts that offers a sense of comfort, a reminder of better days. Then again, on a more practical plane, it may be that country relics cost less money and demand less maintenance than antiques with more aristocratic lineage. The fact is that American Country is a very democratic region of collecting that breeds camaraderie and connoisseurship. If you're smitten by Amish dolls, for example, it's likely you'll find others eager to share your enthusiasm or to trade information. The proliferation of country antiques' journals and clubs has provided a communications system for collectors of every conceivable bent, from advertising tins to Zanesville "sewer pipe" animals. Regional newspapers can be relied upon for candid advice from dealers of good repute, restorers of firm conviction, and collectors with a keen eye on the marketplace.

While some may consider collecting an innocent pastime, an unintentional act, others embrace it heart and soul. Whatever your approach, the experience will be more enriching if you delve into history and keep abreast of current events in every area of collector interest. Linking past with present is, in fact, one of the more satisfying aspects of collecting. To have redware pottery or old cooking tools in your kitchen is a personal connection on two levels. These are not only decorative reminders of colonial ingenuity but also implements that can be employed for daily use.

That brings us to the purpose of this book. For both readers of *American Country,* published in 1980, and those new to my books, *Collecting American Country* serves as a road map for collectors, leading from the challenge of the search through the pride of finding and the joy of ownership. It points out distinctive characteristics for identifying pieces, provides historical information and details of composition, and suggests practical and decorative applications for country furniture and folk art in contemporary homes.

Collecting American Country includes many new reproductions and adaptations of century-old pieces, and thus can be said to bridge the gap between objects made by early settlers and those rediscovered by 20th-century collectors. It describes some familiar and obscure pieces that can be found at flea markets and antiques shops. It defines the regional crafts indigenous to Pennsylvania, New England, the Midwest, the South, and the Southwest, in other words, American Country, and defines many examples of the "incredible miscellany" Dr. Robert Bishop, Director of the Museum of American Folk Art in New York, classifies as folk art: "portraits; genre paintings; textiles including quilts; hooked rugs; needlework pictures and samplers; ships' figureheads; cigar-store Indians; weather vanes; decoys; decorative stone and wooden carvings; pottery; useful household objects; painted and decorated country furniture."

This book does not pretend to cover every aspect of collecting; such an undertaking would require volumes. What it does attempt to do is to span the last three centuries, defining those country objects that qualify as handmade folk art created by unschooled artisans, itinerant craftsmen, resourceful parents, and even children. American Country also encompasses both the hand-hewn and machine-made objects used in colonial households and stocked in general stores. Therefore, *Collecting American Country* includes those items made by early manufacturers whose production techniques enabled them to forge weather vanes, lithograph advertising tins, assemble rocking horses, and mold stoneware pieces by the dozens.

To trace the roots of these country artifacts, the first chapter—Old Things from A to Z—provides a listing of items from the little known to the celebrated that are sought by collectors—as serendipitous an assortment as you would find at any flea market worth its salt. Each entry,

1

accompanied by a photograph, details salient points about the origin of the object and its distinctive traits. This is a cast of characters, so to speak, as many of the objects in Chapter 1 appear in the homes featured on subsequent pages.

Another vital link with the past and an increasingly popular form of collectible is the art produced by contemporary craftsmen who draw on old techniques to weave baskets, make pottery, carve wood, and build furniture. These are the new generation of artisans, admittedly inspired by the anonymous folk artists of the 18th and 19th centuries. Determined to leave their own legacy of folk art, these artists, unlike most of their forebears, are gaining recognition for their individual styles and distinctive mediums. You'll meet some of the artists in Chapter 2—New Things Made by Hand—in which they are shown on their own turf, which may be a borrowed space in their home or in a backyard where creative enterprises are conducted.

Since caring is a concern all collectors have in common, I have devoted Chapter 3—Caring for Country Pieces—to that activity (which can also be called preservation). The material of a piece obviously dictates its care; therefore, each type of artifact receives distinct attention. Professional advice from museum curators and antiques restorers is offered on preserving old paint, protecting aged textiles, maintaining the patina of weathered woods, and a variety of other topics.

Collections can be accent marks or focal points of their environments, depending on how they are displayed. In Chapters 4 and 5, objects are shown in different living quarters where they are treated with ingenuity and respect. Ways to Display and Living with Collections cover modern aesthetics, with specific focus on lighting, hanging, and integrating country pieces into your home, whether that home is a city loft, a landmark house, or a condominium.

The final sections provide additional guidance for collectors. The directories of Contemporary Sources, Antiques Dealers, Periodicals, and Restorers offer names and addresses of reliable sources for new and old country pieces, newspapers and magazines on antiques and collecting, and experts in preservation and restoration.

In the course of researching this book, I, too, have become a collector of anecdotes related by devotees of American Country. One collector, for instance, a literary man adept at collecting his thoughts, attributes his numerous primitive portraits to foraging in the countryside twenty-one years ago when such naïve paintings could be purchased as bargain art. City-dwellers and newlyweds at the time, he and his wife took repeated jaunts to Connecticut where they searched for country pieces that would ultimately furnish an old home in which they hoped to establish roots. As prices for portraits increased, they gravitated to hooked rugs that appealed both to their eye and to their budget. Assured that the dust-laden, tattered rugs could be restored, they made a minimal investment in what turned out to be valuables in a collecting genre. As the supply of old hooked rugs dwindled, they moved on to stoneware jugs, then to painted furniture at rock-

bottom prices. Subsequently, they found a thirteen-room vintage house receptive to their humble but proud possessions. Like so many collectors, they relied on instinct in the course of their hunt. Another collector recalls happening upon a Sunday flea market in a Massachusetts meadow, where a three-foot, hand-forged, electrified copper lighthouse stood like a beacon in the crowd of old trunks and kitchen tools. The curious piece with an illegible signature scratched onto its base excited a love-at-first-sight reaction (which defied any rational explanation). Succumbing to that irresistible urge, the collector negotiated a price in typical flea market style: "Is that the best you can do?" Nevertheless, buying the lighthouse seemed to be an indulgence at the time, one the collector feared was the sign of chronic willpower failure. However, this letter sent by the seller of the lighthouse convinced the collector that her instincts served her well after all: "You'll notice the signature on your lighthouse is that of Eugene Gunn who worked for M. R. Pierce and later for Charles Peck, both plumbing and tinsmiths shops from about 1895 to 1925. I think you'll enjoy it, as it is the only one of its kind." It's this emotional response, that quickened pulse, that Charles Dickens must have had in mind when he wrote: "There is a passion for hunting *something* deeply implanted in the human breast."

Welcome, ye hunters, to American Country!

Old Things from A to Z

To appreciate American Country artifacts *is to understand their origins and their purpose in earlier times. This chapter serves to define those* **furnishings, utilitarian objects, naïve artwork, textiles, and toys** *that have historical importance as well as collecting value. This listing offers collectors* **clues to background, authenticity, and points of distinction.**

ADVERTISING TINS   Late 19th- and early 20th-century lithographed tins are valued for their brightly colored graphics and quaint lettering. The earliest tins, inexpensively mass-produced, were elaborately decorated with scenic pictures and a variety of typefaces, flowers, birds, and borders. They were sturdy, disposable containers for items such as stove polish, gunpowder, and rat poison. Typical shapes were round or binlike. Many pre-1900 products were packaged in what today would be considered economy sizes to hold a six-months' supply of tobacco, coffee, tea, biscuits, and the like.

Decorated tins depicting once-popular products are in great demand now and are therefore escalating in price very rapidly. Even recent tins—those of du Maurier cigarettes and Sir Walter Raleigh pipe tobacco, for example—are steadily rising in value. However, it is possible to find inexpensive examples of these ephemera at country fairs and yard sales. Serious collectors can consult guidebooks for identification and prices.

AMISH DOLLS   The only known toys of Amish children date back to early 19th-century Pennsylvania, Indiana, and Ohio. The humble rag dolls, sewn together with cast-off material, were dressed in the typically plain bonnets, aprons, and capes of the Amish. The dolls were made of solid-color cotton, stuffed with bran, sawdust, or straw. And they were faceless, in accordance with this commandment in Deuteronomy 5:8:

> Thou shalt not make thee any graven image, or any likeness of any thing that is in heaven above, or that is in the earth beneath . . .

In the strictest sects, dolls known as "Swartenruber" were even more primitive in form, fashioned without arms and legs. Dolls with dark faces (only gray or blue cotton was allowed) were also characteristic of these sects.

Authentic Amish dolls are in short supply, since so many of them wore out from constant play. Those that have survived are usually unearthed by quilt collectors who frequent the Amish countryside. Although boy dolls wearing caps and faded denim trousers are considered the rarest, the most desirable old dolls are twins or mother and father figures with characteristic bonnets and capes. For those collectors who discover hatless dolls, miniature bonnets—reproduced to match the originals—may be found at regional antiques shows.

Amish doll sizes range from about 8 to 22 inches; shapes run from skinny to fat with either round pinheads or flat, elongated heads. Occasionally a face will have been playfully penciled in. The more common faceless dolls will often have layers of solid cloth "slipcovered" over their tattered heads. Later Amish dolls, those from the mid-1900s, tend to have softer bodies due to the cotton batting that was used in the stuffing. The quality of stitching and condition of clothing contribute to a doll's worth. However, Amish dolls in almost pristine condition with new-looking clothing may turn out to be recently made reproductions.

ARCHITECTURAL DETAILS

Old columns, corbels, pediments, and gates are but a few of the indoor and outdoor ornaments that have recently assumed new popularity. Collectors are foraging in abandoned houses from other eras, particularly turn-of-the-century gingerbread Victorians, for architectural details that might otherwise be slated for the wrecking crew. The recent interest in classical details for remodeling, restoring, or simply for display, has led to this country-wide search, and a new category of collectibles. Vintage materials range from wood fretwork to iron filigree, weather vanes, and hand-leaded glass panels. Pieces of wood moldings, squares of hand-painted tile, porch balusters, and barn cupolas rate among the favorites. While authentic details are most desirable and worth tracking down at old houses and at demolition sites, modern facsimiles can be purchased from renovator supply companies and through mail-order catalogs that specialize in reproduction trims.

coin or pressing a lever. Some typical forms include a dog with wagging tail; a bear who picks up money dropped from a tree and places it in a box; a monkey with a hat in his hand, which he places on his head. Early mechanical banks were made of cast iron; during World War I, manufacturers used tin and wood to replace the diminished supply of cast iron. While unrestored old mechanical banks can run into thousands of dollars, vintage still banks, though steadily increasing in value, can be found for under $100. For instance, a 4-inch pottery gourd bank sold for $40 in 1982; a metal Mutt and Jeff for $80.

BASKETS

Often referred to as our oldest indigenous craft, American basketry originated with the Indians, who wove food-gathering and storage containers from grasses, bark strands, plant stems, and even roots. The farming colonists adapted the Indian techniques for weaving splint-wood

BANKS

American toy banks, mass-produced to accommodate the first copper coin of 1793, are descended from the money boxes of ancient civilizations. Through the years, banks have been molded out of pottery, glass, tin, and iron in a variety of symbolic shapes, the most enduring of which is the pig (long considered a source of wealth).

"Still" banks, those with no mechanical parts, were the earliest manufactured. These banks, particularly when made of pottery, took the form of hens, chickens, and various fruits, such as those shown above, shapes meant to symbolize fertility and abundance. Great numbers of still tin banks, the most popular of which were in the shape of a house, were turned out by firms such as Stevens and Brown of Connecticut. Initially they were decorated with stenciling and later by lithography. Still banks made of cast iron were also produced in great quantity; those made by the Hubley Company in the 1890s took the form of cash registers and mailboxes. Cartoon characters such as Little Orphan Annie and Mutt and Jeff were the specialty of the Williams Company in Ohio.

Between 1860 and 1935, mechanical banks were produced in great quantity. Designed to amuse children and encourage thrift, their various actions were started by inserting a

9

strips, made from white oak in the southern Appalachians and from ash in New England, into baskets.

Splint baskets are, in fact, the most common (and durable) old variety. Constructed from hand-cut, flexible strips of wood, the roughly textured baskets varied in size and style according to their purpose; for instance, corn-gathering baskets were long, rectangular forms woven into a twill-plaited design, and "buttocks" baskets, which derived their name from their slightly rounded W-shaped bottoms, were designed to carry eggs (some held exactly two dozen). A basket's purpose also determined whether it required a handle, and whether the handle was fixed or movable. Both the corn and the egg baskets had stationary handles, as did the round, ash-splint basket for carrying potatoes. It is the patina and character of a basket's handle that attest to its handwork and age. Wire handles, for instance, probably

mean that a basket was factory-made after the 1880s. Smooth splints (made uniform by machines) and staples are other signs of factory-made baskets. Although few old splint baskets bear identification marks (see Nantucket Lightship Baskets, page 26), some made at Northeastern Shaker settlements in the 19th century can be authenticated by such stamps as "Sabbathday Lake" or "Shaker." Old Shaker baskets represent the best of early craftsmanship, and are characterized by the delicately woven textures of wheat and rye straw.

BEARS Ever since Teddy Roosevelt's bear-hunting incident in 1902, when he allegedly refused to shoot a stray,

his namesake has been America's most popular stuffed toy. "Teddy's Bears" were first produced by Rose and Morris Michtom for their Brooklyn, New York, shop. The enormous popularity of these light-colored plush toys, stuffed with excelsior and embellished with black shoe-button eyes, paved the way for the Michtoms' Ideal Toy Company. From 1903 to 1906, nearly all bears made in America were manufactured by Ideal. Subsequent Teddy bears were made by a number of companies, most famous of which was the German Steiff Company. Bears of this era usually had humped backs, elongated muzzles, and jointed limbs. Black shoe buttons or glass served as eyes. Soft types were stuffed with kapok, while firmer varieties contained wood wool; their black noses and mouths were embroidered. The angora hair of goats was sometimes used to coat the plusher species.

Original Teddy bears, which can cost several hundred dollars, are appealing for their bald spots and tattered limbs—signs of vigorous affection. Commemorative bears, such as the 50th-anniversary Teddy produced by Steiff in 1953 and Ideal's 1978 birthday edition, are considered important collectors' items. Bears made before 1940 fall into the category of valuable antiques. The most popular Teddy bears are those made by Steiff, Ideal, Chad Valley, Schuco, and Shackman. Rare bears may show up at flea markets, garage sales, antique and doll repair shops, or even in trash cans.

Modern versions, which can be purchased for far less than the costly antiques, are potentially collectible also. Unlike their forebears, modern bears have plastic noses and man-made fur. When searching for an antique, it is advisable to visit reputable dealers to study prices and observe the varieties offered. Replaced arms and legs do alter the value of an old Teddy, unless they are closely matched in color and texture. Replacement eyes are acceptable providing they are genuine old buttons or stickpins. For those in search of old bears, a "Wanted to Buy" classified ad may produce the desired collectible. Also, Teddy bear clubs, listed in collectors' publications, provide a reliable source of information for avid bear hunters.

BLACK DOLLS

LACK DOLLS   Since little has been written about black dolls, their origin is difficult to trace. One clue comes from Willa Cather (1873–1947), who wrote in the short story "Sapphira and the Slave Girl" that slave quarters were "littered with old brooms, spades and hoes, and rag dolls and homemade toy wagons of the Negro children." It was the skilled slaves, in fact, who supposedly fashioned dolls for their children and for the offspring of their white masters. Dolls in the image of the "Mammy" were created from salvaged pieces of linen or unbleached cotton. Their heads, sometimes made of rubber nipples or nuts with vegetable-dye-painted faces, were wrapped in traditional bandannas; their bodies covered with homespun dresses and aprons. Often they held white babies in their arms. Mammy dolls, like other racially stereotyped figures, were later made into household objects, such as whisk brooms and doorstops. Like rag dolls, they were cloth-stuffed, or, alternatively, their frames were built of bottles weighted with sand, newspapers, or buckshot. It is the occasional newspaper filling that reveals a doll's actual age.

Although these character dolls were popular during the 1950s, in the 1960s they were frowned upon as civil rights became a national concern. Today, black memorabilia are increasingly important among collectors of folk art that reflects an aspect of American history. Ironically, one particular doll seems to represent a racial blend that was once forbidden: the "topsy-turvy" of Civil War days was comprised of two stuffed linen torsos joined together, one black and the other white. Its roots probably go back to plantation nurseries where black and white children first played together.

CANDLES

ANDLES   In 17th- and 18th-century households, candles were a vital source of illumination, and it was a woman's responsibility to have a large supply of them on hand. The two methods employed to make candles were dipping and molding. The dipping process, one that began at dawn by a roaring fire, required gathering, melting, and purifying animal fat (tallow), then dipping wicks over and over throughout the day until the desired size was formed. For molded candles, wicks were threaded through tubular tin molds and tallow poured in until it hardened. The molds were made in a variety of sizes to hold one candle or dozens of candles at a time.

New England peddlers discovered that the bayberry indigenous to the coastal areas yielded a fragrant wax that could supplement their diminishing supply of tallow. Berries of the so-called candleberry plant were gathered in the fall and boiled in a kettle. After a melting and skimming process, the bayberry took on a transparent green color. Its smokeless and even-burning qualities made bayberry a particularly appealing candle material, as it continues to be for candlemakers today. Beeswax, which provided slow-burning light, was also favored for candlemaking, and many families kept backyard beehives for a steady supply of raw material.

Although the actual colonial candles are etched in history, traditional techniques employed by country candlemakers provide current connoisseurs with an ample supply of beeswax and bayberry types. As for the old metal candle molds, they are valuable memorabilia, as Henry David Thoreau asserted on a visit to Cape Cod in 1849. He wrote: "The pewter molds in which bayberry candles were made can still be unearthed from time to time in antique shops, though they are becoming scarcer by the year." Recently—in 1982—a 6-candle tin was valued at $70, an 18-candle pewter mold with wood frame at $1,000.

CANES Primitive canes, or walking sticks, whittled from tree branches and carved into folk art forms date back to the 6th century. These very personal accessories, often crafted by the individual for himself, usually sport a favorite motif such as a bird, a fist, or a face on their handle. They may be sinuously curved or razor-blade straight; short, average, or long in length, reflecting the measure of the man.

An aura of mystery surrounds most old canes, making them particularly interesting collectors' objects. Although little is known about their origins, the workmanship, particularly for the more formal canes, tells something of the period in which they were crafted. For example, up until the 19th century, most canes bore knot-shaped handles; the crook-shaped handle came into fashion around 1865. Matching canes and umbrellas with carved ivory handles date back to the late 1800s, while canes with carved wood or ivory dog heads as handles represent the Victorian era. Other turn-of-the-century canes were those designed for smokers, some of which contained cigar humidors and cigarettes in their shafts.

The so-called container canes with hollowed-out staves have traditionally been used for all manner of activities, from smuggling contraband to tool-carrying and weapon-hiding. These container canes served 19th-century tradesmen and butter buyers who wanted to appear gentlemanly while toting around their concealed equipment.

Also referred to as gadget, trick, and dual-purpose canes, the container cane was indeed an extension of its owner's trade. Undertakers, for instance, used canes fitted with hooks to close wooden casket containers; photographers carried walking sticks that converted to tripods; itinerant musicians toted music-stand canes from town to town. Canes often aided pranksters with such hidden devices as wolf whistles and water squirters. Other gadget canes catered to tobacco-chewing gentlemen (the spittoon was located in its hollow shaft) and snuff-sniffing females who could reach inside an elegant silver top for grains of tobacco. Canes that concealed weapons are among the more intriguing antiques, for they hid swords, daggers, and knives triggered by push buttons cleverly hidden in decorative handles.

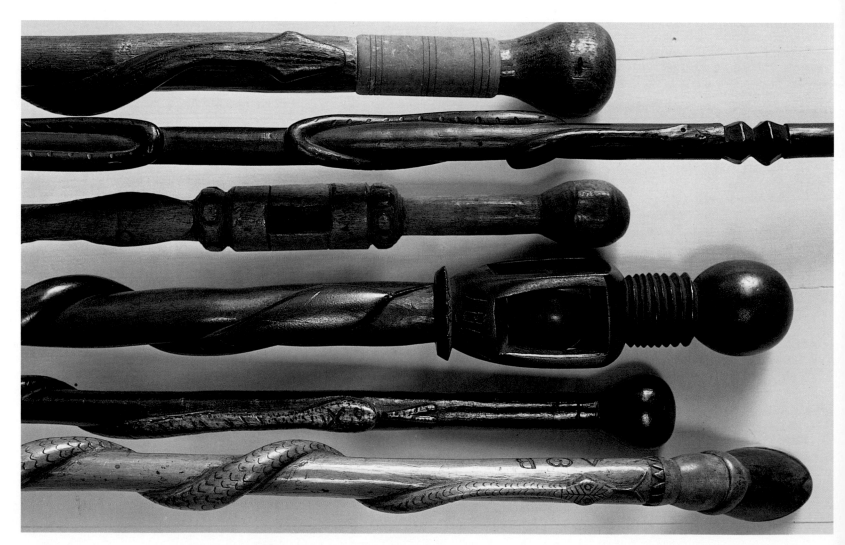

CATS In the *New England Primer*, dated 1688, this verse is recorded: "The cat does play, and after slay." Felines, in fact, have been celebrated throughout the centuries for their impish, mysterious, and even faintly evil qualities. The Chinese were the most prolific producers of cat figurines for export, particularly in the 18th and 19th centuries. This species, cast in porcelain and pottery, is typified by chubby bodies with curled tails and piercing eyes. Similar earthenware cats were made in America, where felines have been a popular subject for artists since colonial times. Many painters in the 1700s created portraits of men and women with cats nestled in their arms. Among the countless 19th-century lithographers who represented cats in a variety of moods were Currier and Ives.

Chalkware cats, bronze or wood sculpted cats, cats depicted in lithographs and wool rugs, and cloth cats are among the wealth of felines created by anonymous American folk artists in the 19th and 20th centuries. The hollow chalkware forms, found mostly in the Pennsylvania Dutch country, New England, Ohio, Indiana, and Michigan, were molded in plaster and vividly painted—a process that originated in Italy. Originally inexpensive

pieces, chalkware cats in good condition are prized collectibles today. Weighty cats, such as those cast in bronze or carved in hardwood, were favorite objects as doorstops in breezy New England seaside homes. These can be found at house auctions along the coast. The hand-painted and stuffed variety shown here originated as bean-bag toys and decorative pillows sewn by the colonists in cotton or linen. Reproductions of the authentic forms can be purchased in kits from craft catalogs and mail-order outlets.

CHESTS American chests date back to the 17th century and have European lineage. The typical chests used for storage of blankets and clothing were sturdy and stout, with bases of oak; decorative trim with carving was usually of maple. A favorite with collectors is the six-board country chest (named for the number of wood pieces that make it up), made from 1700 on. These chests are traditionally constructed of walnut or pine and often decorated with grain-painting in red and black or yellow and brown. The most valuable of the decorated variety, known as dower chests, originated in Virginia, New Jersey, and Pennsylvania. Their embellishment included hand-painted names, dates, figures, and flowers. The authentic—and most desirable—old pieces will have early hardware and telltale signs of wear, including chipped or splintered paint. Construction details will also indicate age. Before 1800, chests often used interlocking pieces of wrought iron as hinges (called snipe hinges) and were put together with crude nails. Square-headed cut nails and butt hinges usually are marks of craftsmanship dating from 1830 on. Wire nails, modern screws, and steel hinges are signs of repair or later vintage.

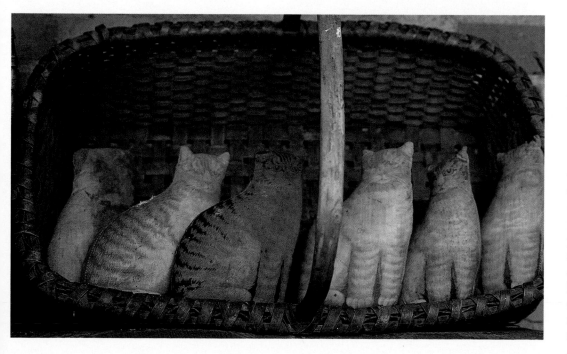

13

CHILDREN'S FURNITURE

Diminutive furnishings held fascination for both children and adults in the 18th and early 19th centuries. The majority of these small-scale objects were created expressly for children; however, some of the pieces that have come down to us today as children's furniture are actually thought to have originated as tradesmen's samples, which were transported from town to town in wagons or strapped to tradesmen's backs, or as examples crafted by apprentices in the furniture trade to illustrate their skill.

Simple country pieces, counterparts of full-size furniture, were produced in Philadelphia, Connecticut, and Western Pennsylvania, where woods of pine, elm, walnut, oak, ash, and maple provided material for local cabinetmakers. Baby ladder-backs, children's Windsor chairs, tables, and chests typify the American-made country pieces of the late 1700s. Little rocking chairs, particularly the Boston rocker painted in black and yellow with stenciled border scenes, were sometimes signed by the craftsman. Many of the early American pieces were plain wood; however, some received fresh coats of brick-red or blue-green paint with freehand decoration created by parents for their offspring. Another form of decoration developed about 1815, when new types of machinery enabled cabinetmakers to spool-turn woods, stained or painted, depending on the attractiveness of the natural color. Among the appealing features of children's furniture are their signs of youthful wear and tear; for instance, chairs that were constantly dragged across floors will have smoothed edges on their legs, or table surfaces may occasionally be marked with initials in a childlike hand.

CIGAR-STORE INDIANS   The ancestry of advertising dates back to the 1700s, when manufacturers of patent medicines were touted in local papers. Subsequent developments in advertising were trade cards, vegetable crates, and shop signs. Perhaps the most familiar memento of an advertising ploy is the cigar-store Indian. During the years from 1850 to 1890, these hand-carved figures of chiefs and maidens were placed outside tobacco shops to attract passersby. The nearly life-sized Indians were exposed to all weather conditions; many were destroyed by the elements or fire in the course of their vigil. Other Indian figures stood inside shops on top of a table or counter. These commoner varieties were 2 or 3 feet high and made of iron, wood, or plaster of Paris.

A few hundred authentic figures remain and are in great demand among collectors. Because of the rarity and popularity of the Indian figures, many reproductions have been created in the same hand-carved manner.

CLOTHESPINS

Along with wash buckets and scrubbing sticks, clothespins were born out of necessity in the early 19th century. These primitive laundry articles, which were once purely utilitarian, are now nostalgically considered decorative objects, valued for their simple craftsmanship and age. One of the most fundamental and useful of the implements employed daily was the clothespin. Like other aged woodenware, the humble clothespin often showed distinctive signs of being hand-hewn: no two were exactly alike. Carved out of fallen tree limbs and scraps of pine, cherry, and oak, the first clothespins had either roughly squared or rounded tops with two tapered prongs, resembling the bottom half of a stick figure. Some were banded with a thin piece of tin that could slide up and down the shaft to tighten the grip.

Originally made in New England and at the Shaker community in Ohio, clothespins ranged from 3 to 4 inches long and varied in width according to the carver's style. By the late 19th century, they were uniformly made and mass-produced in factories. Those few that survived fires and trash heaps have been spotted at country fairs and antiques shops specializing in old kitchenware.

COOKIE CUTTERS

With the Industrial Revolution of the 1830s came mass production of metal kitchen equipment, which included a wide range of cutting utensils. Each gadget was designed to perform a particular task, from mincing meat or vegetables to carving dough into specific shapes. The fluted cookie cutter, for instance, was used regularly to make simple sugar cookies, a favorite to this day. It is still manufactured in its basic, round shape with a small handle. Another type of cutter, one with a revolving cutting form, was made of aluminum and tin in 1915. Rolled across a sheet of dough, it would stamp out uniformly round cookies. A round cookie cutter, made in Chicago around the same time, carried this embossed advertisement: "White Lily Flour Has No Equal."

Both plain and fancy cookie and biscuit cutters were made from scraps of tin at home or by traveling tinsmiths. Typical shapes consisted of animals, flowers, or hearts. An old cutter can usually be authenticated by spot-soldering marks.

DECOYS

The making of decoys shares a place with basketry as the earliest native American craft. Like baskets, decoys are traced back to the Indians, who devised lifelike replicas out of mud, stones, feathers, and grass to lure wildfowl. The device was adapted by New England settlers in search of food. These early birds, carved from white cedar or pine, bore only a slight resemblance to wildfowl; however, they managed to lure young migrants from Northern breeding grounds. More realistic decoys with painted plumage began to appear in the 1840s and 1850s.

Carving a perfect replica required an instinctive knowledge of wildfowl and four major steps: body-making, head-making, assembling, and painting. Rigging consisted of attaching ballast and an anchor, and fastening (weights and anchors varied depending on the region and carver). Among the more prized decoys are those regional types indigenous to the eastern seaboard, particularly New Jersey and New England.

During the late 19th and early 20th centuries, there was no limit to the number of birds a hunter could shoot and thousands of decoys were produced, most of them along the Atlantic coast and Mississippi River flyways. But ever since conservation laws were first imposed in the early 1900s, hand-carved decoys of all species have lured flocks of collectors.

DOLLHOUSE FURNITURE

Toy companies whose specialty was creating furniture for dollhouses were first established in the early 20th century. Among the major firms were R. Bliss Manufacturing Company, Tynietoy of Rhode Island, and Schoenhut of Philadelphia. Great detail was lavished on some of the miniature pieces, such as the replicas of Sheraton, Chippendale, and Hepplewhite furniture made by Tynietoy. Miniature pianos were among the first pieces produced by toy companies; they were followed by highboys, four-poster beds, painted chests, chairs, and tiny accessories that added elements of realism to the room settings. Tynietoy's craftsmen duplicated in fine detail the English and colonial styles fashionable during the 1920s and 1930s. Many of those pieces are identifiable by the firm's name on the base. Schoenhut's designs were noted for simple, sturdy lines. Bliss built its reputation on high-quality lithography of details on paper and wood in both dollhouses and furnishings.

DOORSTOPS

These ornamental weights, otherwise known as door porters, replaced purely functional stones and bricks used to hold doors open. The earliest designs appeared around 1810 and were round, cast brass forms with long wooden handles for moving them about. In addition to painted or bronzed cast iron, other doorstop materials were earthenware, hand-carved wood, marble, and inexpensive green glass (the squat, dome shapes made in England, known as dumps). The wide variety of doorstops produced before 1920, and most sought after by connoisseurs, fall into two general types: those in the form of animals and those representing an important person or event of the day. Heavyweight brass dogs and flower baskets, Indians, and sporting and folk figures were typical of this era.

The most desirable doorstops still have their original—preferably unchipped—paint. Pieces that have been retouched do not necessarily diminish in value, if they are very unusual. Vintage doorstops can be found through ads in collectors' periodicals, at flea markets featuring metal objects, and at estate auctions of 19th-century homes.

EMBROIDERY

In the late 18th and early 19th centuries, women's academies instructed young women in the art of stitchery, examples of which are to be found in embroidered tablecloths, pillowcases, guest towels, and samplers. The decorative handwork was accomplished with cotton, silk, wool, silver, or gold threads on cloths, leather, and even paper. During Victorian times, white embroidery on a white ground became popular.

Although elaborate stitchery is highly valued in certain European embroidery, the most sought-after American needlework is the modest embroidery from the 18th and 19th centuries that falls in the category of simple folk art. These embroideries include

samplers, which were showpieces for young people's decorative techniques; mourning pictures—stitched representations of weeping-willow trees, urn-shaped memorials, and figures—which are often signed and dated; and show towels, illustrated above, which were white or beige linen towels placed over everyday towels when guests were expected. Embellished with monograms, alphabets, and motifs such as birds, hearts, or silhouettes, show towels were characteristically embroidered in red or blue thread.

FIREPLACE TOOLS
The early American hearth was a central heating zone and the forerunner of our modern kitchen range. It was equipped with a full complement of tools for preparing meals and tending the fire. Andirons, tongs, brush, poker, shovel, and tool boy—all typically made of iron and brass—stood next to the fireplace. Wrought-iron utensil racks, hung by the hearth, often held such 18th-century necessities as a large spoon, spatula, skimmer, and flesh fork (for holding meat). Their handles were elongated and usually unadorned; their function purely utilitarian.

FLASKS First produced around 1800, flasks were narrow-necked containers meant to hold liquids—and whiskey in particular. In the flask-making process, hot globs of glass were inserted in molds, then blown into somewhat uniform bottles of pint and quart sizes. The original pocket-shaped flasks also date from this time; hundreds of these flasks, filled with liquor, were sold or passed around during political rallies. Typical motifs on vintage flasks include patriotic slogans or likenesses of political figures, such as Washington and Adams. Flowers, trees, animals, and birds—various motifs from the realm of nature—also appeared. Historical flasks range upward from $35 into the hundreds for the rarest varieties, and many private collections are stored in vaults.

FRACTUR Named after the 16th-century typeface, a fractur was an illuminated family document, hand-lettered by a schoolmaster, local minister, or itinerant penman of German descent. Records of merit, as well as marriage, birth, baptismal, and death certificates, were lettered and then gaily bordered with watercolor designs. Elaborately tinted decorations incorporated flowers, birds, and angels on fractur of the late 1700s (considered extremely valuable). Later examples, those made in the mid-19th century, had text reproduced by lithograph and open borders for hand decoration. By 1900, both text and decoration were produced entirely by photographic printing processes. Often stored in the family Bible, fractur provides colorful genealogies of settlers who migrated to Pennsylvania, Ohio, North Carolina, Indiana, and Texas.

GRANITEWARE A relative of tinware, which was made predominantly of iron, graniteware (also known as agateware) was so called because of its speckled or swirled patterns characteristic of these rocks. In the late 19th century, factories produced great quantities of this kitchen and bath ware, cut from sheet iron coated with a porcelainlike material. Cups, soap dishes, coffeepots, and all manner of plates and pans resulted. These pieces are notable for their country charm, often associated with picnics and campfires. The typical background color is white, with swirls of gray, green, blue, red, or yellow.

Graniteware, as well as all tinware, originated in the Northeast along the waterways where the raw material was plentiful. Since tinsmiths migrated from New England in summer to southerly locations in winter, examples of their craft

are widespread (and moderately priced). Collectors seek to assemble whole sets of desired color combinations in good condition. Bent or chipped surfaces are common flaws in much of the old tinware, but some collectors are willing to accept these character marks as an indication of honest service.

HEARTS

Objects of affection, hearts have cast their spell on generations of collectors, and it appears that they have been coveted throughout American history. Women of the 18th and 19th centuries sewed pincushions in the shape of hearts from scraps of taffeta, silk, or satin. One yellow silk heart-shaped cushion, supposedly made by Martha Washington, sold at auction in 1975 for $400. Hearts were also a favorite motif for kitchen implements, such as molds, cutters, and waffle irons. Often a blacksmith would finish off a utensil with a heart-shaped finial or handle. Furniture, too, was embellished with cutout or painted hearts. Early banister-back chairs, stools, and benches frequently were bestowed with heart decoration. Valentines, of course, captured a major share of hearts and continue to do so. (See Valentines, page 36.)

IRONSTONE Opaque white china, inspired by European wares, was first produced by Andrew Duche of Savannah, Georgia, from 1740 to 1743. It became more widely known as "stone china," made by Josiah Spode II. Patented in 1813 by C. J. Mason, it achieved great popularity and was frequently imitated. Commercial ware referred to as hotel china first appeared around 1885. From 1890 to 1900, other names synonymous with the heavy grade china were white granite, opaque porcelain, and flint china. The earliest pieces to appear in America, though, were high-priced English patterns known as Gaudy Ironstone,

HOOKED RUGS With woolen, cotton, and linen remnants from their dressmaking, colonial New England women either hooked or braided rag rugs. The simple hooking process involved securing unknotted and unsewn loops in a piece of linen or canvas. The loops were held in place by pressure against one another; the greater the number of loops per square inch, the more durable the piece. The finest examples may have as many as 20 loops per square inch. Age is difficult to determine, although there is occasionally a date hooked into the rug. However, that date may refer to a historical event that occurred long before the rug was hooked.

Designs incorporated into the rugs consisted of pictorials (animals, ships, houses, and landscapes) or commemorative events. The animal motifs are most common and the historical designs most rare.

A craze for hooked rugs in the 1920s and 1930s depleted the supply in many a country attic and barn. Consequently, finding good examples requires perseverance. Those rugs that haven't faded from wear and tear might have been created with fabrics in the brighter, more durable hues associated with the mid- to late 19th century. Most hooked rugs were round or oval in shape, backed with jute or burlap.

popular in the 1840–1860 period. Heavy and durable, it lived up to its name; most patterns were densely flowered, with accents of bright colors and gold. The Gaudy Ironstone range included approximately 25 patterns. From 1870 to 1890, patterns tended to be plainer, such as Cable and Ring. Among the marked all-white ironstone are patterns called Lustre Sprig and Lustre Pinwheel. However, much of the white ironstone bears no marking at all.

JARS

Glass jars have long been in widespread use as storage containers for food and beverages. Beginning in the early 1800s, they were mass-produced in glass factories, with particular condiments or beverages determining their design. For instance, pickle and pepper sauce jars (produced during the 1800s in New England factories) were usually green or aqua and often had Gothic arch embossing; thus they became known as "cathedral bottles" in the wider category of "Pic Jares." In the early 19th century, airtight jars for preserving vegetables and fruit made their appearance, mass-produced by Mason and Ball, the New England Glass Bottle Company. A later 19th-century arrival, designated for milk storage, was the bottle embossed with farmers milking cows, or with birds, buildings, or other appealing designs. About 1855, the widemouth canning jar with a tin lid was invented. And the mason jar with its revolutionary screw top (patented in 1858 by New Jersey tinsmith John Mason) was the forerunner of modern fruit jars. Their zinc tops were fitted with threads to match the molded glass. Jars with proper lids are considered more valuable than those without.

KACHINA DOLLS

Among the Hopi and Zuñi Indian tribes of Northeastern Arizona and New Mexico, the kachinas are believed to be gods living in the snow and ice of mountain peaks. The belief holds that the gods, embodied in man, come down to the villages to receive prayers and distribute gifts. These gods are also thought to control weather, particularly rainfall.

In the manner of Father Christmas, the kachina is believed to bring dolls to Pueblo girls, bows and arrows to the boys. This custom is thought to instill religious beliefs and ensure that rituals will be carried out during certain seasons. Dolls representing the gods are used in religious rites and then passed on to Indian children.

Dolls and their masks are made from cottonwood, which the Indians carve and rub with sandstone. The Hopi dolls, brilliantly colored, and the whitened Zuñi dolls, may be decorated with feathers, twigs, cornhusks, or deerskin, depending upon which god they represent. There are kachinas for all seasons, and for flowers, birds, snakes, and symbols related to hearth and home. The square-looking forms have either separate, removable masks or attached masks that were carved as part of the body. In Hopi dwellings, native kachinas are usually displayed on white adobe walls along with handwoven rugs and dried herbs.

Unlike the Hopi, the Zuñi people secrete their kachina dolls; they are not commercially available to tourists. Those kachinas that fill roadside stands near Indian reservations are among the thousands of Hopi-made dolls sold as souvenirs, not to be mistaken for the actual dolls used for religious rites and the amusement of Indian children.

KITCHEN UTENSILS

KITCHEN UTENSILS   A domestic history of America might be written based on kitchen utensils. The profusion of antique apple parers, for instance, speaks of the popularity of apples in American homes. Throughout the early and mid-1800s many parers were handmade of wood modeled after Moses Coates's patented device, invented in 1803: the apple was secured on prongs and rotated against a blade. Wood gave way to mass-produced cast iron by the 1850s. The first rotary eggbeater was patented in 1870; cast-iron models were crude but graceful ancestors of the motorized metal or plastic beaters popular today.

The most desirable collectible kitchen tools are those that reflect changes in the American life-style. During the late 1800s, the rural housewife prepared and preserved food with the help of kitchen gadgets, such as nutmeg graters, sugar cutters, raisin seeders, and nutcrackers. Since many of the devices she used were retired long ago, some guesswork may be required to identify them now. Today, many of these primitive, outmoded utensils are amassed by collectors to hang like sculpture on modern kitchen walls. Old kitchenware is readily found at country flea markets, where prices may range from $7 for a 1903 cast-iron rotary beater to $35 for an 1882 apple parer.

23

LAMPS Eighteenth-century lamps, both the hanging and standing variety, consisted of a round or oval oil-holder and a cloth wick. Most common of these early lighting devices were Betty lamps, made of wrought iron or steel and manufactured in Pennsylvania. Of Swiss and German origin, Betty lamps were often marked with their makers' names. Derr, Eby, and Hurxthal, for instance, are prized names among lamp collectors. As of 1787, whale-oil lamps made of tin, pewter, or brass became popular. Glass versions appeared in the 1820s, manufactured by leading firms such as the New England Glass Company and the Sandwich Glass Company. Their whale-oil lamps in a variety of patterns are avidly collected. Both glass and metal went into the making of lamps that burned kerosene, the refined fuel introduced in the mid-1800s. Gone With the Wind lamps (lamps with one or two hand-painted glass shades) and Aladdin lamps (with glass chimneys and simple round metal bases) are favorite collectibles of this genre.

Early American lanterns, most often used on carriages, were candle holders encased in either wood or tin. Certain tin types were cone-shaped and pierced for decoration. At first, the lanterns contained panes of shatterproof horn, then isinglass, and finally glass. The currently popular lighting in the American country style includes old crocks that have been converted into lamps and topped with homespun or pin-cut paper shades, reproduction tin candle lamps, and reproduction kerosene lamps.

MOLDS To shape and provide decorative form to a variety of foods as well as candles, colonial women counted molds among their frequently used kitchen tools. Some 19th-century tin molds primitively modeled after animals and birds appear to have been handmade. These molds resemble cookie cutters in their flat, sharp-edged, and simple forms. The deeper metal molds often

had fluted sides and lids with decorative motifs in relief. For instance, the fluted tin-lined copper molds used for steaming puddings had separate covers embellished with raised fruit designs.

Molds made of wood (treenware) were used to imprint designs on butter, maple sugar, cookies, and jellies. These 19th-century molds were usually carved from birch or pine and bore fruit, leaf, and animal motifs. Today, they are sought after by collectors for their regional flavor (often Pennsylvania Dutch) and distinctive folk carvings. (See also Candles, page 11.)

MORTARS AND PESTLES

During the 1800s, each New England community had a cooper who made functional items such as barrels, buckets, molds, and kitchen tools of wood. Mortars and pestles were among the many tools he produced. These ancestors of the food processor were crafted of maple or pine for the most part; however, for mortars of early American vintage, iron, brass, marble, and ironstone were used as well. Pestles, also known as beetles or mashers, were employed to tenderize meat and mash potatoes, spices, and grain.

The mortar and pestle also served as a symbol for apothecary shops (modeled after chemists' signs in England), where they were regularly used by doctors and druggists in the preparation of medicines.

MOUSETRAPS Although the first mousetrap was not patented until 1864, many lethal devices for catching mice were employed long before. Spring-type traps owe their origin to crude but effective handmade wood boxes which were designed to entrap rodents who frequented colonial houses. One design imprisoned mice in a wooden chamber reached via a trapdoor; as mice entered the contraption, the door would shut, forcing the animals into a larger chamber where wire loops dropped down, making escape impossible. It was then up to the trapper to decide the fate of his captives. A more expedient trap contained an iron blade in a guillotinelike device fitted inside a wood box. A mouse met its end while pursuing the bait. The price a collector pays is considerably less; an 1800s wood mousetrap runs between $28 and $35 (1981 flea market quote). Older spring-type models are in the $2 range.

NANTUCKET LIGHTSHIP BASKETS Woven principally of rattan brought home by sailors returning from the Orient, these baskets deserve their own category because of their distinct origins and the outstanding durability of their design and composition. Named for the lightship established at South Shoal, Nantucket, in 1853, they are thought to be the handiwork of the Quakers, many of whom moved to Nantucket at the height of the whaling industry. The baskets, made on molds, were round or oval with tightly woven bodies, turn-board bottoms, and split-ash swing handles. Many were signed and dated by their craftsmen.

Most prized are the nested baskets, usually made in groups of eight, with the smallest pint size, the largest 12-quart size. The sturdy Nantucket Lightship baskets were originally used for a variety of chores, from carting potatoes, firewood, and fish to storing knitting materials. This rhyme, a trademark from the late 1800s, attests to the baskets' endurance:

I was made on Nantucket.
I'm strong and I'm stout.
Don't lose me or burn me,
And I'll never wear out.

Within the last fifty years, another Nantucket basket has evolved—one with a cover and decorated with ivory carvings of whales or various types of fish. Known as friendship baskets, these covered varieties are typically used for handbags. Since the traditional basket is still being produced, well-preserved old baskets may be confused with new ones. Because there is such a craze for Nantucket baskets, prices are at an all-time high, and collectors had best make sure they are buying the genuine article.

friendly looking impostors used for luring ducks. Owl replicas (some of them stuffed, others carved) attracted their supreme enemies, crows, that would flock to harass and taunt them. The crow became fair game for target practice, while the stern-faced owl stared on. It has been speculated that the owl's usefulness to farmers may have contributed to its reputation for wisdom, as it did away with squirrels, rats, mice, and other rodents who preyed on crops and grains.

PANTRY BOXES   The colonial kitchen was a veritable storehouse of containers, and pantry boxes (also known as firkins) were perhaps the most versatile since they were constructed to hold daily necessities—pills and butter, grains and spices. Eighteenth- and 19th-century carpenters supplied households with handcrafted boxes of graduated sizes before factories began to stamp out graduated canisters of tin, wood, and then plastic. The round or oval pantry box was usually made of ash, maple, or pine. Other woods, particularly beech, birch, and hickory, were often combined in the construction.

The earliest boxes have telltale marks of the carpenter's craft, such as thick, shaped laps, mixed woods, and multifaceted nails. An incised date or owner's name also characterizes vintage antique boxes. In the 1820s, carpenters such as Jonathan Loomis of Whately, Massachusetts, sold fine quality pantry boxes for 50¢ each. Today's collector is more likely to find factory-made versions from the late 19th century, inspired by sturdily constructed Shaker boxes. The Shakers' handcrafted pantry boxes included painted finishes of bright red, yellow, blue, or green, sometimes ornamented with grain-painting or sponging. Nested boxes, favored as decorative stacks in the 20th century, were valued in colonial times for their storage capacity, most commonly for spices. Authentic original boxes of this sort may still have a lingering fragrance of cinnamon, nutmeg, or ginger—evidence of prior service.

OWLS   The wise old owl has enjoyed a long history since its image was stamped on the first Athenian coins of ancient Greece. In American folk art, it has served in a variety of roles from wood ornaments for banisters to decoys to painted cardboard decorations for Halloween. Owls as decoys worked on a different principle from the

PEWTER   Also known as poor man's silver, pewter was used daily in many colonial keeping rooms, dining rooms, and kitchens. When highly polished, the tin alloy material does bear a strong resemblance to silver; however, its more common patina is a rustic, oxidized gray. English pewter was gracefully crafted in a fine alloy of tin with copper and antimony. American pewter-smiths evolved their own unpretentious designs with a similar subtle gray appearance. Early pieces of colonial pewter that bear the worker's initials, hometown, or motto are among the most valuable examples of marked American pewter. Since pewter was fragile by nature, it required construction similar to silver—casting or handwork. During the early 19th century a "hard metal" pewter, known as Britannia ware in England, was introduced to America. Small factories grew from pewter shops, where standardized Britannia ware could be produced.

Early pewter tableware—porringers, tankards, plates, bowls, platters, teapots, coffeepots, and cutlery—were intended to withstand frequent scourings; therefore little decoration was bestowed on these purely functional objects. When ornamentation was employed, it took the form of beading or reeded edgings to emphasize fine curves and elegant proportions, imitating fine silver. Some later pieces were engraved after casting, but deep engraving seldom appeared.

The American pewter industry flourished after the Revolution and up until the Civil War. It is the pieces from this period—those influenced in design by contemporary silver —that most appeal to collectors of Americana. Another less expensive area of interest is the wide variety of household items fashioned in Victorian factory-made pewter. Authentic pewter is discernible by its heavy weight and resonant tone when struck.

PORTRAITS   Folk art portraiture was created in the 1800s by unschooled itinerant painters who roamed the hinterlands of New England and the Midwest. These art peddlers, also known as limners (from "luminaire" or "illuminate"), were usually graduates of a trade such as sign painting, gilding, or house painting, and their work was typically flat and without shadows. Primitive painting thrived during the late 18th and early 19th centuries when scores of anonymous artists would prepare costumed bodies on canvas during winter months, and in the spring set out with their stock to hunt for customers. Patrons would then choose appropriate finery from a painter's inventory, and the painter would provide a relatively realistic head for a decoratively dressed torso. The portraits were done on whatever materials were available—wood panels, canvas, or even ticking   and were typically painted in oil, although watercolors and pastels are also known.

QUILTS

QUILTS Like so many other colonial crafts, quilting was born of necessity. Intended to warm beds in chilly rooms, quilts were conceived with a sandwich construction designed to insulate. Whether one-piece, patchwork, or appliquéd, they had three essential components: a top layer, filler, and lining, or bottom layer. The earliest American quilts were made of solid colored pieces of cloth held together with running stitches.

Eighteenth-century quilting bees, high points in the lives of prospective brides and festive occasions for housewives and children, produced a variety of designs, from solid, stitched coverlets to more elaborate pieced and appliquéd quilts made of cotton or sometimes wool. Multiple patterned borders and central motifs, such as a Tree of Life or a vase of flowers, were popular before 1850; later 19th-century quilts were usually abstract geometric patterns pieced together from everyday fabrics with fine stitchery.

Designs of Victorian vintage (late 19th century) called upon more serendipitous scraps such as velvet, silk brocade, and satin

for the crazy quilts and lap robes fashionable in that era. During this period the quilts were often too fragile for bed coverings and began to serve more decorative purposes as throws for furniture or pianos. After 1900, many quilts were machine-stitched in a tight, even pattern in contrast to the freehand stitch of earlier specimens. Quilt kits, which appeared in 1935, produced standardized designs with precut fabrics.

Since all types of designs were produced during several historical periods, fabric is the most dependable indicator of a quilt's age.

For instance, calicoes and ginghams were popular fabrics prior to 1870, as were floral chintzes and indigo-blue prints. When aniline dyes were introduced in the 1870s, brighter hues of red and green appeared. Some quilts tell of their particular history by names and dates stitched into corners, linings, or tops. Such quilt patterns as "Birds in Air," "Lone Star," "Drunkard's Path," "Robbing Peter to Pay Paul," "Kansas Troubles," and "Star of Bethlehem" suggest that examples of this native American craft were as colorful in content as in design.

want-not period of American history are these rag balls of vegetable-dyed cotton used by the Amish when stitching their simple clothing and dolls.

RAG BALLS

RAG BALLS   Rather than pile scraps of fabric in storage boxes, colonial women wound leftover strips into round forms like rubber-band balls. When material was needed for patching clothes or making rag rugs or dolls, the balls were handy to unravel. Characteristic of this waste-not,

REDWARE

REDWARE   The same red clay used for bricks and roof tiles went into redware, America's oldest native pottery. Quantities of utilitarian redware crocks, jugs, and bowls were made for the colonies. The inexpensive, fragile earthenware often was decorated with sgraffito (incised designs) or slip (designs poured on the surface). Slip-decorated redware is referred to as slipware. Redware has been a popular collectible since the turn of the century and is now sold at a premium, with highest prices commanded for pieces that are sgraffito-decorated. As an example of redware's value in the collectors' marketplace, a 6-inch plate with yellow slip decoration sold for $150 in 1982; a 6-inch brown speckled mug for $65.

REVERSE PAINTINGS

REVERSE PAINTINGS   Just as the term suggests, this kind of artwork was executed in reverse. Specifically, paint was applied to the back of glass in a reversed process, beginning first with highlights, then middle tones, and ending finally with grounds. The art, a particularly frustrating one, required great patience and competence. In the 1850s, the Pennsylvania Germans were the first Americans to master the technique, which originated in the Orient and was adapted by various European countries. Celebrated political figures, such as Daniel Webster and George Washington, were favored subjects in reverse painted portraits. Winsome girls, flamboyantly dressed and coiffed, were also popular depictions. That their tiny bud mouths were curiously similar suggested these were stock designs painted by itinerant artists whose work was rarely signed.

ROCKING HORSES　After the Revolution, hobbyhorses crudely crafted of wood became common playthings for American children. A clue to their popularity is in this 1785 advertisement run by a Philadelphia cabinetmaker:

Rocking horses in the neatest and best manner, to teach children to ride and to give them a wholesome and pleasing exercise.

While some of the more primitive designs were boatlike shapes with carved horses' heads, realistic examples often appeared in the nurseries of fine old homes. Steeds of aristocratic bearing, for instance, might be half life-sized, carved with flaring nostrils, dappled flanks, and real horsehair tails and manes. The classic hobbyhorse, made in the mid-1900s, was carved from wood, painted, and set on curved rockers.

SANTAS   In colonial New York, the Dutch Saint Nicholas was modified to Santa Claus, who supposedly could slip down chimneys, backpack and all, in a sootproof suit. This magical creature has inspired all manner of figurines, in chalk, glazed pottery, cast metal, carved wood, and glass. The most common Santa Claus figures had clasped hands, a bag of gifts, or a Christmas tree over one shoulder. Chalk Santas frequently held a real sprig of evergreen. In the late 19th and early 20th centuries, various manufacturers of pottery, chalkware, paper products, and Christmas tree ornaments produced new commemorative Santas each year; limited in numbers, these Santas are particularly desirable.

SCRIMSHAW   Though frequently faked in reproductions, authentic scrimshaw is, in fact, carved whalebone that has been engraved or scratched with a design. The craft originated with American sailors whose long trips to the South Pacific, Alaska, and Africa inspired their designs, while allowing them enough leisure time to perform such painstakingly detailed work.

Scrimshaw's most prolific period coincided with the height of the whaling trade, from 1820 to 1890. After a whale was killed, the bones were removed and doled out to the crew, who scraped them clean and smoothed them with sandpaper or sharkskin. Ashes from the ship's fire served as polishing material. The decoration then followed,

either scratched in crude freehand (for particularly valuable types of scrimshaw), or applied in set patterns. Patterned decoration was most common; it involved pasting cutout pictures on a bone's surface and then pinpricking a portion of the pattern to be incorporated into the design. The finished line work would then be darkened by rubbing India ink or grease into the scratches. Silver, mother-of-pearl inlay, or wooden fittings were sometimes added to scrimshaw intended as a special gift.

SQUEAK TOYS
More commonly known as pipsqueaks, these toys originated in Europe and were adapted in America during the 19th century, particularly in Pennsylvania. The animal toys of painted papier-mâché emitted sounds somewhat appropriate to their species—by sheepskin, cloth, or paper bellows that squeaked when pressed together. Extremely popular as

Christmas gifts, they appeared under the tree in a wide range of characters, usually mounted on wooden bases.

In addition to squeaking, some toys were also set in motion by a squeeze of the bellows: birds on spring-coiled legs bobbed around or flapped their wings; the tongue of a lamb would pop out. Because of their frequent use and fragility, old pipsqueaks tend to be in poor condition; however, occasionally, a well-preserved piece turns up —to the delight of a keen collector.

33

decorative reliefs of hearts, flowers, and geometric designs, plus brass tacks, bits of glass, and lithographed pictures.

By 1900, men and boys throughout America were making a variety of objects using the tramp art technique. Among the objects crafted were dollhouse furniture, boxes, sofas, chests of drawers, and tables. Powered jigsaws, according to the markings on 20th-century tramp art, were employed. This craft all but vanished when people began to work in factories after World War II, and leisure time was used differently. Since tramp art was made by anonymous craftsmen, the pieces bear no signatures, but a revealing date may appear on a cigar box or fruit crate. Since its recent recognition, this curious folk art form has steadily appreciated in value, with a doll chest of drawers, made of cigar boxes, selling for $65 in 1981, and a corner shelf, with chip-carved edges and applied ornaments, for $175.

TRUNKS   Forerunners of the modern suitcase, traveling trunks, some of which were covered with cowhide and studded with nailheads, like the examples shown here, were widely used during the stagecoach days. These varied from cashbox size to ample proportions, and often had tops connected by leather hinges. Many such trunks were lined with newspaper or wallpaper. Brass or iron nailheads sometimes spelled out a monogram on the top; the interior was frequently embellished with the owner's name as well as a diary of his trip. Tin trunks, which had domed or flat tops, some with lithographs on their lids, were used after the Civil War by 19th-century travelers. These trunks turn up at country sales and auctions and, like traveling trunks, can still be acquired at reasonable prices.

TRAMP ART   Attributed to itinerant workers who traveled the Northeast in search of odd jobs, tramp art was composed of layered wood sheets, whittled and shaped to create an illusion of depth. Old cigar boxes were the usual medium, supposedly chosen by immigrant craftsmen who came here in droves from Europe after the Civil War. Tramp art was actually based on chip-carving (or notching), a technique practiced in Europe, especially Germany, during the 16th century. The construction is characterized by nailing, or gluing together, layers of thin board from dismantled cigar boxes or fruit crates made of soft wood and easy to come by. A three-dimensional quality, which could otherwise be achieved only by carving, was accomplished by graduating the shape and size of each layer. Small notches were carved from the layers of board for additional interest. Since there were infinite ways to layer and notch pieces together, no two examples of tramp art are identical. In addition to layering and chip-carving, tramp art is often embellished with

UNCLE SAMS   One story about the origin of the name Uncle Sam tells of a butcher, Samuel Wilson from Troy, New York, who supplied meat to the U.S. Army during the War of 1812. He also held a job inspecting Army supplies, and was so well thought of that no one questioned his integrity. As the story goes, Uncle Sam, as he was called by neighborhood children, stamped the acceptable supplies with "U.S.," which became known as "Uncle Sam's Stamp of Approval." Cartoonists and artists picked up the nickname and created Uncle Sam characters, the most famous of which was depicted in the posters inviting young men to enlist in the Army.

Sam Wilson's actual appearance remains a mystery, but his caricature has become universal. The white-whiskered gentleman with a tall, thin body and striped hat has inspired myriad folk art forms, from banks and wind toys to star-spangled woodcuts.

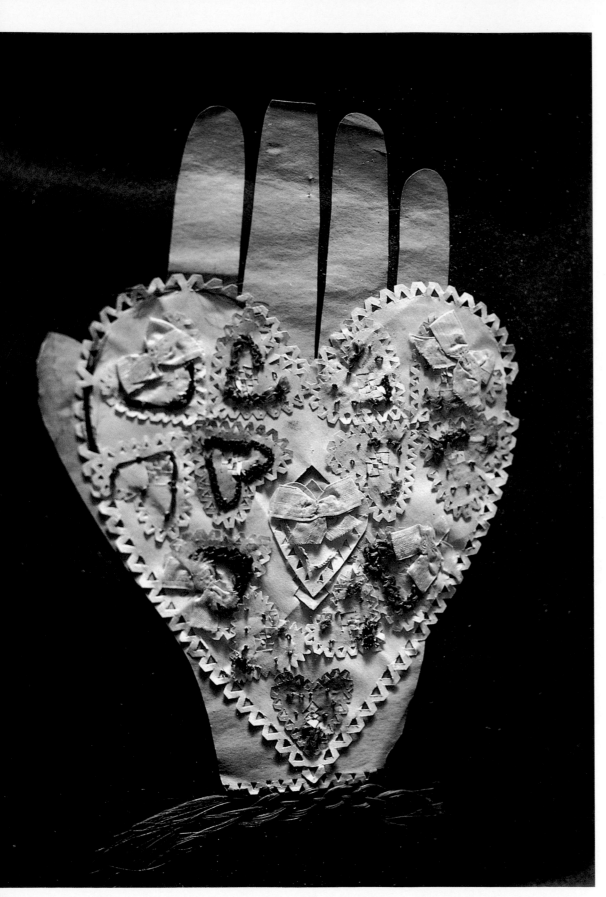

VALENTINES Expressions of sentiment were handwritten by America's early settlers, who continued the amorous celebration of St. Valentine's Day. The first mass-appeal valentines were produced at the end of the 18th century. Comic types and those with movable parts followed in the next century.

Rarest of the valentines are the original handmade ones, although the commercially produced cards, particularly those lacy, delicate renditions from 19th-century England, are greatly valued for their delicate beauty. Certain 1800s handmade valentines fall into the category of folk art: the intricate openwork designs cut from paper with scissors; the stenciled designs created with watercolors applied through the openwork of stencils cut from oilpapers (known as theorem paintings); and sailors' valentines, which were wood frames or boxes trimmed with shells. Other very collectible cards of a later date are those depicting uniformed soldiers from both world wars, sailors with sweethearts, and three-dimensional stand-ups made of ballooned honeycomb paper.

The major American manufacturer of commercial cards was Esther Howland, who shipped ornate designs all over the country from her Worcester, Massachusetts, home. A small red H identified most of her pastel cards from 1848 to the mid-1870s, when her firm became the New England Valentines Company. Valentine seekers also look for the names of Jotham, Taft, T. W. Strong, and Berlin & Jones, all known for their lacy valentines of brightly colored papers.

WASHBOARDS Forerunner of the push-button machine, the early washboard was hand-carved of wood with a ridged center. This fundamental tool received its U.S. patent in 1833 when clothes were scrubbed in buckets and handcrafted for that purpose alone. Subsequent versions of the simple board had separate rollers held

tightly in a rectangular wood frame. Some rollers revolved, others were immobile. Factory-made washboards often had uniform corrugated wood centers, or, alternatively, scrubbing surfaces constructed of rows of spools, quite like spool posts. Washboards could also be made of wood frames with ridged pottery centers. Of the old washboards sought by collectors, the glazed pottery board with a sponge or spatter design is particularly popular.

WEATHER VANES The primitive forms that in the early 1800s first earned their keep on roofs of barns, cottages, and cupolas were America's earliest weather forecasters. These wind-sensitive instruments were commonly in the shape of domestic animals, such as cows, roosters, and horses. Banners, pennants, and arrows were usually seen on public buildings and churches; fish, mythological creatures, patriotic symbols, and trade emblems were other popular motifs.

Before 1850, weather vanes were three-dimensional figures handmade of hammered sheet copper; however, few examples from this era exist outside folk art museums. Factory-made vanes, from the late 19th and early 20th centuries, are what most collectors hope to find: three-dimensional copper forms, measuring about 2 feet in length, that were hammered into shape in iron molds, then trimmed and soldered into one piece, and often covered with gold leaf. Those copper vanes manufactured by Cushing and White of Waltham, Massachusetts, identified by the firm's stamp, are highly prized. Weather vanes with cast zinc heads, heavier than hollow copper, were molded by another Massachusetts firm, I. Howard Company.

Simpler vanes—and more common than the three-dimensional designs—are sheet-iron silhouettes cut in the form of farm animals, banners, or arrows. Reproductions of all types of weather vanes, some actually made from surviving 19th-century molds, often mimic the originals so closely they are difficult to distinguish. Nevertheless, a greenish patina on copper and traces of gold leaf (especially on the underside) suggest old age. File marks on seams also indicate age, since 19th-century craftsmen filed away excess solder in the course of finishing points. Clever counterfeiters, though, manage to simulate many of the character marks, including corrosion and bullet holes (weather vanes were likely targets for sharpshooters).

Over the last 50 years, museum representatives and private collectors have combed the countryside for enviable examples of weather vanes. The search is best conducted at barns in the back country where old vanes originated: New England, Pennsylvania, Ohio, Michigan, and Northern New York State, or through reputable antiques dealers. Country roads are also good hunting grounds for these coveted antiques, some of which may still be stationed atop isolated barns and may possibly be for sale. Unfortunately, because of the increasing value placed on old vanes, they have become fair game for rustlers who have been known to swoop down in helicopters, snatching them off rooftops.

WHIMSEYS   Usually made from a single piece of wood, whimseys were carvings meant to entertain, puzzle, or exhibit a craftsman's skills. Many examples of these whittlings made at the whim of their creator represent a high level of craftsmanship and ingenuity. One favorite among wood-carvers was a ball enclosed in a cage, whittled as a grand display of dexterity. Whimseys also took the form of miniature farm tools, such as the spindly grain cradle that has been described as the "Stradivarius of early American farm implements." Whimseys, like early toys and handmade whirligigs, are most often found on back roads and at country auctions.

WHIRLIGIGS   An animated relative of the weather vane, whirligigs, also known as wind toys, once stood on porch rails and fence posts, their movable parts set in motion by wind currents. Hand-carved wooden figures with paddlelike arms were the earliest examples from the mid- to late 1800s. The variety of forms range from simple shapes sawed from wood planks to complex mechanisms with rotating windmills and figures with flailing arms. Unlike weather vanes, these whimsical toys provided entertainment for adults and children. Frequently they were carved and painted by amateur craftsmen for pleasure or for gifts. Wind toys, like weather vanes, are rare antiques that have inspired a rash of reproductions. Many contemporary renditions are handmade in the manner of early 19th-century craftsmen—and are collected as amusements and folk art facsimiles.

X   This letter is collectible in the form of wooden alphabet blocks originally made in the 1850s by immigrant wood-carvers. "X" was hand-painted, lithographed, cut out, or embossed on sets of alphabet blocks that were intended to teach children their XYZs.

Among the earliest blocks commercially produced in America were those that featured upper-case letters on one side and lower-case letters on the other. Originally made by the S. L. Hill Company, letter blocks were packed as sets in wooden containers.

Since whole sets were broken up in the course of a child's play, collectors often track down individual letters to build a significant assortment. "X" marks the collector's choice in this case.

Y

ELLOWWARE This earthenware, made from a type of New Jersey clay that yellows as it fires, is most commonly found in pitchers and bowls. Pieces may vary from light tan shades to rich pumpkin. In the late 19th century, graduated four- and five-piece sets of mixing bowls were added to the basic, mostly undecorated forms. Favorite examples of yellowware are banded in shades of brown and white, and matching sets of bowls, ranging from a mere 3 inches to an ample 24 inches around, are particularly desirable.

Less common yellowware pieces include molds, custard cups, rolling pins, pie plates, and serving dishes. For the collector with a limited budget, common yellowware is an ideal category, especially those pieces made by the prestigious Bennington Potters of Vermont, one of the first American producers. A sample price in 1982: a 7½-inch mixing bowl with relief exterior, $25.

Z

ANESVILLE "SEWER PIPE" ANIMALS These novel forms of pottery were made from the late 1800s to the 1940s by workers after hours in the factories of Zanesville, Ohio, where sewer pipe tiles were made. Using leftover clay mixed with shale, the unschooled artisans tried their hands at sculpting clay, firing it in the factory kilns that reached 2,000 degrees. The clay forms were then salt-glazed, a process that involved shoveling salt into the kilns at the peak of their heat; as the salt vaporized and settled on the objects, a clear glaze built up.

While sewer pipe animals were undistinguished for artistic merit when they were first made, these curious-looking clay figures have since achieved stature as regional folk art, which some collectors find appealing today.

"The uglier they are, the better they seem," says Jack Adamson, a Zoar, Ohio, antiques dealer and a collector of sewer pipe animals. His book on the subject, *The Illustrated Handbook of Sewer Pipe Folk Art,* validates the Zanesville sewer pipe craft as true folk art, notable for its unique character and humble origins.

New Things Made by Hand

*A renewed respect for handmade pieces has stimulated a renaissance in the crafts. Here are some **worthy examples of recently made folk art and furniture** that are inspired by models from the American past. While these collectibles may not have the monetary worth of 17th-, 18th-, and 19th-century pieces, they nonetheless display the **appealing handcrafted quality and honest simplicity** of country antiques.*

As antique pieces grow more scarce and more expensive, good new work fills the void. These expressions of American ingenuity are finely crafted substitutes for out-of-reach antiques: they are unpretentious

REDWARE PLATES AND BOWLS *(preceding pages)* **line the studio of potter Lester Breininger.**

PRIMITIVE PAINTINGS AND SCULPTURES *(left and right),* **including animal portraits, watermelons, decoys, carved pigs, sheep, and a Liberty figure, are displayed in a store. These original signed pieces do not parade as antiques but rather as examples of 20th-century crafts.**

artworks made by rural craftsmen with their own hands in their own homes as a hobby or as a vocation.

Twentieth-century crafts cover a range of cottage industries, from carving apples or making herbal wreaths to furniture-making, basketry, pottery, primitive sculpture and paintings. What all these endeavors have in common is their handmade character. And they have an air of familiarity in their naïve shapes, primary colors, and natural materials. Most are based on tried-and-true techniques. For instance, woods are worked in the old-fashioned manner and bear marks of the carver's knife; baskets, made of seasoned splints, are woven according to standards set forth by colonial craftsmen; pottery made from native clay is Old World in style, as are

Shaker-type chairs, decoys, and simple toys.

The craftspeople whose work we have chosen to present in this chapter are outstanding too. Unlike their colonial counterparts, these modern artisans have achieved recognition and are rewarded for their efforts by loyal patrons who delight in finding a unique piece signed by a living artist.

EARTHENWARE

Pottery made in the Southeastern Pennsylvania workshop of Lester Breininger has a long history. This ninth-generation Berks County Dutchman models his wares in a century-old tradition, using locally dug clay and antique molds. To perfect his methods, Lester studies past work of local potters, conducting research through old newspapers, assessment records, and even cemetery records.

The procedure for making a redware plate, for instance, consists of first mixing the clay to an even consistency and smoothing it out with a rolling pin like pie dough. To achieve the desired texture, Lester allows the clay to freeze and thaw during winter, storing it in bathtubs for that purpose. He cuts disks from the weathered clay, then "slams" them onto molds for drying. Slip decoration, or "trailing," is done at this stage. The process is a quick one that involves pouring liquid clay (slip) through goose quills so that it leaves a trail of color in a free pattern. "You have to work quickly," says the potter, "because if you don't keep moving, the slip will pour into a big puddle." This spontaneity produces free-form designs that typify slipware. A more restrained technique is that of sgraffito, or incised designs. In the Breininger workshop, this traditional art is practiced by Lester's wife, Barbara.

POTTERY *(left)* forms in the hands of Lester Breininger.

HEART PLATE *(top right)* made of "slip-trailed" redware and sgraffito.

NAMEPLATE *(right)* is the most personalized form of pottery.

ROWS OF REDWARE *(below)* show a potter's repertoire of ornamented bowls.

HEARTS, FLOWERS, AND RURAL CRAFTS

Holly Meier's infatuation with America's early folk arts has developed into a full-time commitment to an at-home antiques business. However, her Connecticut farmhouse also bears witness to a love for crafts. Holly's handmade artwork includes floorcloths and cut lampshades—two forms of Americana she interpreted from 18th- and 19th-century designs. Like pioneer artisans who learned by doing, Holly cut her stencil patterns for floorcloths in heart, flower, and house motifs, then painted different-sized canvases with acrylic colors.

As for her cutout lampshades, they were inspired by the perforated tin lantern reputedly carried by Paul Revere on his midnight rides. Holly's renditions, cut out of heavy, parchment-colored paper, are pictorial, based on scenes from the Meier farm.

CUT-PAPER LAMPSHADE (left) has been stenciled in farmyard motifs.

SCENTED HEARTS (above), made from fabric remnants, are stuffed with herbs and spices.

PAINTED FLOORCLOTHS (right) are coated with polyurethane.

Herbs are dear to Holly Meier's heart. She has, in fact, woven wreaths of many herb species in the shape of a heart, a symbol she relates to very strongly. "It's my trademark," says Holly. "I've collected hearts ever since I was fifteen." Holly's passion for things heart-shaped appears in myriad forms, from pillows to wreaths scented with a cluster of fresh or dried herbs.

The source of her plentiful supply is a Connecticut farmyard herb garden (heart-shaped). Here flourish mint, rosemary, lavender, tarragon, sage, lemon thyme, and oregano.

Herbal wreath-making grew from a desire to handcraft gifts for family and friends. This creative pastime has turned into a family event, as children pick fresh crops, father forms and solders wire frames, and mother trims the herbs. Holly's wreaths, round or heart-shaped, range from a mere 2 inches to a generous 5 feet. To secure the herbs to their frames, she uses fine wire, frequently decorating her creations with hand-dyed ribbon.

Since the herbs are freshly picked, wreaths start out in greens of the garden, eventually drying to earth shades. Gradually, Holly claims, "they lose their aroma and become quite brittle." Because of their limited life, she makes fresh wreaths each year.

Throughout the year, the Meiers' farmhouse wears wreaths—in closets, on bedroom doors, and even in bathrooms. The spicy-sweet scent refreshing each room can be traced to a solitary wreath or a grouping of herbal forms. Holly's advice to other wreath enthusiasts: "Experiment . . . try different combinations of herbs and dried flowers. There are no rights or wrongs, just have fun!"

HERBAL WREATHS are hung like a series of picture frames in orderly rows. Dried grass, flowers, willow, and juniper contribute silver and earth tones to this assortment made from round or heart-shaped forms. Some are trimmed with ribbons.

SHAKER-INSPIRED FURNITURE

The chairs Ian Ingersoll builds are firmly rooted in two solid traditions: Shaker and Scandinavian. This contemporary craftsman is scholarly in his approach, guided by the late 18th-century Shaker designs of Robert Wagan and the 20th-century chairs of Danish architect Hans Wegner.

Ian worked at making "freestanding furniture" because he couldn't afford to buy Shaker antiques and found reproductions lacking in comfort. He took to studying Shaker workmanship through historical data recorded about the Mount Lebanon, New York, colony (where Robert Wagan perfected the post and rung rocker). Ian's modern chairs are direct descendants of the simple sturdy designs born in Mount Lebanon and the spare, finely crafted chairs of Hans Wegner. Devising his own blueprints, Ian labored four years to perfect chairs that are predominantly maple, but occasionally cherry.

The rocking chairs made in Ian's workshop are, he says, "such exact reproductions of the Shaker rocker, it is hard to tell the difference." Indeed, Ingersoll rockers boast such Shaker trademarks as woven tape seats, pointed finials, and top, or "shawl," rails originally used to suspend a cushion.

After studying historic manuscripts describing "steambend jugs, arm forms, and patterns," Ian designed machinery to assure authentic reproduction. His goal: "A dining chair that would be comfortable to sit in for at least four hours."

STRAIGHT-BACK CHAIR *(left)* with woven tape seat conforms to the Shaker dictum "Beauty rests on utility."

ROCKERS AND DINING CHAIRS *(below)* respect both Shaker and Scandinavian designs in their straightforward lines and hand-stained finishes.

MUSHROOM CAP *(above)* is an authentic ornament on the arms of late 18th-century Shaker chairs, hand-turned in a modern workshop.

FRESH WREATHS

For craftswoman Kathy Killip, the outdoors is a natural resource that fuels her creativity. "I began making wreaths for a garden club demonstration, to show how you can go out into the fields and gather all kinds of herbs, grasses, and vines." Kathy's resourcefulness is usually at work during car trips; she stops on country roads to collect nature's bounty of wild brush, then tames it into fresh wreaths. Her historical reference goes back to Rome, where wreaths were symbols of victory, and to American pioneers whose cornhusk wreaths celebrated an abundant harvest.

From her point of view, the wreath is a "continuous circle, a circle of friendship and love, something that is special enough to hang on a wall or door all year long."

Kathy, who launched her wreaths at Renaissance fairs near her Midwest home, uses only natural materials in their construction. Bases are formed of wild grapevine, buckbrush, or willow. To this she adds greenbrier, wild rose, sage, buckwheat, and roadside pickings.

That her craft bears a kinship to folk art is no coincidence. She is an avid collector of Americana, which, she claims, is a decorative influence in both wreath-making and pottery—another enterprise.

NATURAL WREATHS are made of wild brush and vines.

ARRANGEMENTS

Although her arrangements are newly made, Doris Stauble of Wiscasset, Maine, taps a cache of antique material for her one-of-a-kind creations. She attributes her success to a lucky discovery: an old factory filled with dressmaker and millinery trimmings. Without having any plans for the contents, she gradually acquired them anyway.

"I had an idea that there was something I could do with the lovely old silk fruit, flowers, and leaves. I thought they would somehow go well with the antiques I sold in my shop." What she did was to arrange artistically the trimmings in old baskets; those that were seriously faded, she restored with dye. Doris makes each unusual arrangement individually with her precious supply of old-time materials, filling in with occasional pieces of papier-mâché. Her work has attracted numerous clients from all over the United States.

ALL THE TRIMMINGS from an old hat factory are reunited in one-of-a-kind arrangements.

53

NANTUCKET LIGHTSHIP BASKETS NOWADAYS

Newly made Nantucket Lightship baskets link past with present; the high standards established more than a century ago are maintained today. Among the current makers of collector-quality baskets is Bill Sevrens, whose work was inspired by Mitchell Ray, grandson of Nantucket's prolific 19th-century basket-maker. Bill attributes his craft to an apprenticeship with Ray, for whom he worked from 1921 to 1933.

Referring to himself as "the last of the old-timers," Bill describes the basketmaking sequence (about thirty-five hours' worth of labor). First, he makes splints and staves from pliable green oak, then sets them on a mold to dry for about a week. After weaving, he attaches white oak handles with brass rivets. Finally a thin coat of varnish is applied.

Bill signs his baskets on the inside; next to his signature he glues a penny to authenticate the year.

Following the pattern of his own training, Bill employs apprentices who are taught the "old-timer's way." They work year-round in a renovated stable by his house, filling orders from every state. Bill receives high praise from fellow Nantucketer and avid Lightship basket collector Norman Kaufman, who portrays the Sevrens baskets as "sturdy, well-made, and graceful." Furthermore, they improve with age.

NEW NANTUCKET BASKETS are handmade according to 19th-century techniques. They are woven in graduated sizes and frequently collected in nests.

PAINTED FIGURES

Lou Shifferl, like his father, is a self-taught artist whose rural upbringing instilled in him an interest in simple forms and rustic textures. For more than twenty years, Lou has collected folk art, particularly decoys, and has studied historical work housed in regional museums.

Most of his materials are old fragments he can salvage rather than buy, such as wood pilings, fence posts, siding, and tin. Using the most fundamental tools—a hand ax, rasp, and files—this carver creates fanciful shapes as a hobby. The vintage quality of his owls, eagles, shorebirds, and whirligigs is particularly convincing because of the weathered materials he recycles and the sincerity of his work. His painted figures indicate a strong color sensitivity and skilled hand.

Lou's talent as a painter of rural scenes in the American Country genre is widely recognized. Says collector Barbara Johnson, who features his originals in her Rockford, Illinois, shop, "Lou is extremely talented at carving, equally so at painting, and it takes a combination of both for quality work. There are a lot of carvers who cannot paint; the painting is what makes this work special." She goes on to define this new breed of folk art as "basically a nonacademic expression of a person's talents in creating something by hand. Good workmanship of any handmade piece—whether it is two hundred years old or made yesterday —reflects the talents of its maker. Many hours of labor went into each piece, and that's what gives it the beauty, warmth, and charm we admire."

ANIMALS, ANGELS, AND OTHER FOLK ART

Modeling clay was Nancy Gardner Thomas's first medium. She recalls her childhood years in postwar Germany when clay was doled out to "keep the children quiet." Although Nancy was adept at molding miniature animals and produce, it wasn't until she reached forty that her handicraft developed into what is now highly regarded folk art. Her sculpture, in fact, has recently reached the White House—in the form of 65 Christmas tree ornaments.

Nancy's commercial involvement with crafts began as a risk-taking venture upon leaving her secretarial job in Virginia, "to do what I wanted to do." Encouraged by a friend who commissioned a carved bird, Nancy experimented with a variety of materials such as wood putty ("like molding clay"), tin, rope, and straw, plus stains and acrylics.

Nancy's métier, she points out, is not duplicating old folk art. "I don't want to emulate it, but to make my own designs from ideas in my head."

She favors soft woods for carving, specifically pine and poplar. And to maintain the personal quality of her artwork, Nancy produces certain pieces in limited editions. Because of the demand for her ornaments, the artist has increased that particular supply with the assistance of a woodcutter and her own daughter, who meticulously applies the paint.

ANIMAL PAINTINGS *(above),* **oil on canvas, represent a cow, two pigs' heads, and a cow's head.**

CARVED SWAN *(above)* acts as a signpost for a rural antiques shop. It is perched on weathered wood, encircled with metal.

ELEVATED RAM *(left)* is depicted in realistic detail; its body is made of shaved wood to resemble fur.

ANIMALS AND ANGELS *(below)* are two of Nancy Gardner Thomas's trademarks. Animals are mounted on wood bases with wheels similar to old-fashioned pull toys. Wood shavings for wings give her "flying" angels texture.

IMAGINATIVE FOLK ART is Nancy Gardner Thomas's forte. To keep up with the demand for her carvings, Nancy has turned a hobby into a full-time endeavor. Here she's at work in her Virginia studio making limited editions and mass-produced crafts.

FOLK ART FIGURES *(left)* wear the black hats and simple garb of Amish men. Artist Sherman Hensal draws on memory and a keen eye for detail to create realistic figures replete with carved and painted clothes.

BASKETS OF VEGETABLES *(below)* could easily be a garden variety of nature's produce, but, in fact, are scraps of wood carved and painted to mimic the real thing.

BREADS AND PIES *(bottom)* are homemade—not in a bakery, but in a craft workshop where softwood and household paints are the ingredients.

TRUE-TO-LIFE CARVINGS

As a change of pace from teaching junior high school science, Sherman Hensal decided to produce vegetables at his home. With the help of his wife and son, his crops have grown abundant, but not by way of conventional gardening.

"I've never had a green thumb," he explains, "and I can't grow a thing. So I figured I just better carve 'em."

That led to an artistic enterprise which has proven to be very fruitful. Sherman's carving actually dates back to boyhood. "Since I never had many toys, I started carving for my own amusement. I'd make a tree root into a gun or boat," he recalls.

There is still a playful quality about his work; in an attempt to fool the eye and the appetite, Sherman "raises" vegetables and fruit that would do nature proud. His repertoire of edibles extends to baked goods—pies and breads that appear to be fresh from the oven. They, like all his other objects, are carved of soft redwood or scraps.

To achieve authenticity of texture and color, Sherman studies his subject, then spends hours refining the finish. Because there is no formula for specific colors, each new batch of cantaloupes, for instance, will vary from the previous crop. Also, Sherman's carvings include figures—simple ones inspired by Amish folk—and a menagerie of animal forms.

FACE JUGS

Face jugs, according to Burlon Craig, are derived from Africa, where they were supposedly placed on graves to ward off evil spirits. As his explanation goes, it was the African slaves who introduced face jugs to America. They became a traditional Southern form of folk art, indigenous to Georgia and North Carolina.

Burlon makes face jugs in his North Carolina pottery shop with a style that is entirely his own. "I dig the gray stoneware clay," he says, "and grind it in my pug mill. Then I turn the clay on a kick wheel." Referring to himself as the last of the old generation of potters who still makes stoneware this way, Burlon uses glazing techniques that involve pulverizing scrap glass, clay slip, and wood ashes.

Burlon's kiln, which he burns three or four times a year, holds up to 500 different-sized pieces of pottery, so his output can be substantial. In addition to face jugs, he produces a variety of jars fired in the 12-foot by 24-foot kiln that gets heated to 3,000 degrees with pine slabs from the sawmill.

FACE JUGS *(left)* are gray stoneware before being glazed.

AT THE WHEEL *(below)* potter Burlon Craig prepares his clay.

THE FINISHED PRODUCT *(right)* after firing and glazing techniques were employed.

A CARPENTER'S SCULPTURE

Felipe Archuleta works at home in Tesuque, New Mexico, where he began carving fifteen years ago during a slack period in his carpentry business. This award-winning artist attributes his creativity to "divine inspiration," and to the help of his son Leroy, one of seven children. Archuleta's self-taught carving techniques produce forms that are hailed by contemporary folk art enthusiasts and gallery owners from New Mexico to New York, Paris, and Tokyo.

His favorite materials are native cottonwood for torsos and Chinese elm mostly for limbs. He will only use dead wood, as greenwood will crack in the drying process. With the aid of a chain saw, he cuts the soft material to desired working size, then chops it into rough shape. Whittling the features comes next, followed by sanding and the application of common house paint, either exterior enamel or latex.

Archuleta's creations come from observing the forms and markings of animals, and sometimes from the shape of raw wood. He has received steady encouragement from the art community ever since the International Folk Art Museum of Santa Fe first exhibited his work in 1972. He was the recipient of the 1979 Governor's Award for excellence and achievement in the arts of his home state of New Mexico.

CARVER AND SON *(above)* practice their art outside their Tesuque, New Mexico, home.

UNIQUE SPECIES *(far left)* of Felipe Archuleta's are considered museum-quality folk art in America and abroad.

ANIMAL KINGDOM *(below)* was carved of soft cottonwood, inspired by photographs and shapes of wood in its natural state.

DECOYS

Byron Bruffee was lured into decoy-making by his father, who took him along on hunting and fishing expeditions. As a child he learned to repair the decoys of experienced hunters, eventually carving his own versions to replace those worn out by continual use. As decoys became more popular among folk art collectors, Byron employed his carving techniques to meet the demand. He's become a full-time decoy-maker whose range includes about 30 different species produced in his Massachusetts studio.

Byron uses a band saw to cut rough outlines of his decoys, then rasps the wood. Sanding and painting follow. His past experience as a hunter provides mental images of the wild-fowl and fish he re-creates.

DECOYS IN THE MAKING (above) are carved by Byron Bruffee, who favors white cedar found in New England swamps.

FISH AND FOWL (left) are oil-painted as were old decoys used by hunters. These contemporary carvings, however, are designed exclusively as ornaments.

TWIG FURNITURE

The whimsical, bent forms commonly called twig furniture are probably country cousins of the rustic garden furniture made from tree roots in mid-18th-century England. In both cases the actual craftsmen are unknown. These free-form furnishings, like folktales, have evolved in the course of history, their makers as anonymous as the forests that provide broken limbs for their structure. The majority of all rustic American furniture was originally constructed for use in the late 19th- and early 20th-century summer camps throughout the Northeast and South. Many of the camps in New York's Adirondacks owned by the captains of industry were furnished with twig pieces. However, the spot most renowned for the style was the Old Faithful Inn, built in the early 1900s in Wyoming's Yellowstone National Park.

Contoured rustic chairs were production-made in the Appalachians around 1890. These bentwood styles, fashioned of willow, hickory, or maple, often formed with basketry techniques, are still being made by mountain craftsmen according to their own visions of design. Usually, the twig's natural curves and distortions dictate a shape: however, greenwood may be bent into a variety of configurations.

TWIG CHAIRS, handmade by a North Carolina craftsman, offer outdoor nesting places for Jonathan and Samantha Emmerling.

NEW WAYS WITH OLD WOOD

Every piece that Barbara Kelley makes is tagged with this message: "Our contemporary American Folk Art evolved from a lifelong passion for primitive antiques and nostalgia for New England seacoast villages during the early colonial period." It goes on to state: "We strive for authenticity in our art, for we represent a heritage and a spirit for American people."

Both Barbara and her husband, Bob, have a vested interest in the new generation of folk art; they strive to produce quality work that will appreciate in value on the basis of its artistic merit and individuality.

The Kelleys approach their craft as a team, he as the carver and she the painter. To give each piece a timeworn character, they search for naturally weathered woods along the Santa Fe Trail in their native New Mexico and on back roads of Pennsylvania and Ohio.

The carving is a freehand process; therefore, no two pieces are identical. Painting requires a repetition of sanding and coloring to achieve an honestly distressed finish. Frequently this takes as many as five processes before a piece has been finished satisfactorily.

The Kelleys' assortment of old-looking folk art consists of pull toys made from salvaged wood (one horse is fashioned from a discarded croquet mallet), farm animals, and Western and nautical figures.

WOODEN SAILORS *(left)* **include old wind toys, or whirligigs, with paddle arms and the Kelleys' contemporary renderings. Other carvings echo colonial weather vanes and decoys.**

FOLK FORMS *(below)* **stand in the Kelleys' window. These familiar silhouettes are mounted on blocks of wood for display; they owe their distressed finishes to modern craft.**

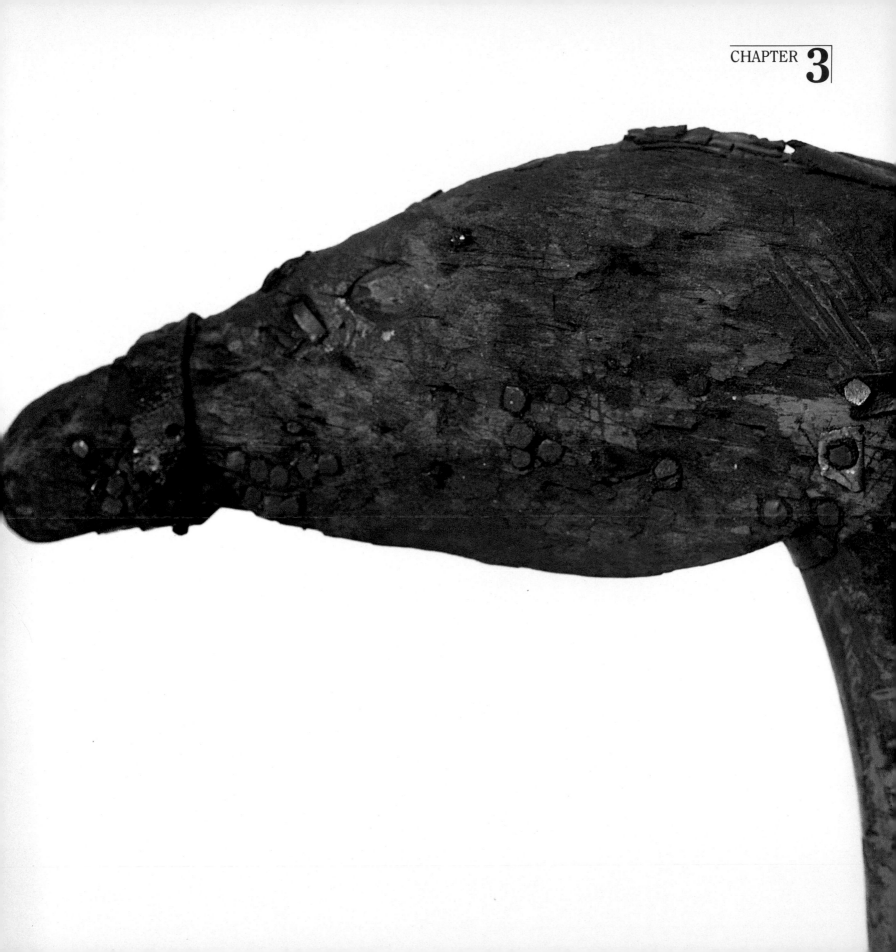

Caring for Country Pieces

*Preserve is the credo of every antiques enthusiast—and the point of this chapter. Whether to rid an old metal piece of rust, polish aged wood, clean a century-old quilt, or leave well enough alone are typical questions that crop up in the course of collecting. With **insight from knowledgeable collectors and restorers** of wood, textiles, metal, and ceramics, we offer **some caring advice.***

Like so many other endeavors, the art of caring for country pieces requires sensitivity and knowledge. Volumes of sophisticated recommendations may offer no more useful preservation techniques than the simple words of advice "Handle gently to avoid the need for repairs." When dealing with ceramics, for instance, always handle an antique piece at the widest part of its base,

using two hands to lift it; do not immerse a cracked or previously repaired piece in water or solvents, and do not coat surfaces with oils or varnishes in an attempt to shine them. Avoiding hazardous conditions minimizes elaborate repair work.

But there are do's and don'ts in dealing with old wood, metal, and cloth, and guidelines are presented here. An important aspect of care is

cleaning, which offers protection against the elements and aging.

Caring for certain old pieces includes living with the blemishes that age imposes. However, when objects of particular value demand repair, a restorer should be consulted.

HORSES' HEADS *(preceding pages)*, restored and unrestored, represent two attitudes toward antiques.

WIRED CROCK *(far left)* was restored in a primitive fashion to prevent a crack from splitting the ceramic in half. The wiring, probably done in the early 1900s, is a mark of distinction.

CERAMICS *(left)* bear slight chips— acceptable marks of antiquity.

THE CONDITION OF THINGS

"Some people only like things pristine and perfect," says collector Jerry Smith, who prefers the charm of certain worn pieces. But, he maintains, "it takes a sensitive eye to differentiate between junk and antique." While the extent of an antique's wear and tear is not necessarily his prime consideration, Jerry steadfastly avoids old objects suffering from dry rot or bugs, no

LIBERTY FIGURE *(above)* is from a boathouse in New Hampshire. In exceptionally fine condition, the piece has its original paint and professionally restored ears.

BLACK CARVING *(left),* 18 inches high, is presumed to be a carnival piece in its original condition. Indoor climate is controlled to preserve the old wood and prevent paint from peeling.

matter how reasonable the price.

Another noted collector places great importance on the condition of a piece. One exception is if an item is very rare, in which case its condition may be to some extent overlooked. An example is the cement Indian sculpture shown here. Obviously aged by years of exposure, it is valued for its rugged character and uniqueness. Since this 1,000-pound figure was meant to live outdoors, it sustains the vicissitudes of the weather with little concern on the part of the owner.

CIGAR-STORE INDIAN *(above)* **is a century old. Once an outdoor object, this wood piece now resides in a collector's home where it receives an occasional dusting.**

CEMENT INDIAN SCULPTURE *(left)* **was made by Ohio bricklayer Noble Stuart. A hardy figure, he is undaunted by weather and survives on little attention.**

SIGNS OF AGE

The original condition of a country piece, however crude, is often the barometer of its worth. For that reason, a collector should be able to identify age through certain telltale signs. Woodenware, for example, shrinks as it ages, causing box tops

and bottoms to draw away from veneer sides, knots to fall out of wood surfaces, or round bowls to become somewhat oval. Wooden pegs and wrought nails indicate age, as does a light velvety smooth patina—the result of years of handling. Sometimes peering inside and underneath an object enables you to find such clues to its age. Aged paint is characterized by a hard, spidery texture, worn away in spots. Paint that's been distressed to look old would be more evenly distributed and less subtle.

Repairs, too, are common earmarks of age, and reputable dealers should be forthright when a piece bears signs of restoration. Since wooden objects were so highly valued in the past,

repair work was often a measure taken to extend their usefulness. Therefore, old restoration (and work) is a form of caring that should be acknowledged.

CANE SEATS *(far left)*, 1870s, were originally carried to cockfights as canes, then unfolded to provide spectators with a perch. The fact that cane seats had three legs and fragile proportions suggests that they were damage-prone. However, the leg and seat detail of this piece *(above)* reveals a well-preserved specimen.

NEW ENGLAND BOX *(left)*, from the 18th century, wears its original coat of milk paint faded with age.

ANTIQUE SLEDS *(left and center right)* date back to the turn of the century and were produced by two major companies, Flexible Flyer of Philadelphia and the Paris Sled Company of South Paris, Maine. Those with painted surfaces intact are most desirable. Sled authority Bill Carhart recommends the following care to preserve original paint:

Rub wood gently with waterless hand soap; wipe with paper towels. Stop when dirt is removed or when there are traces of paint on the towel.

Apply a coat of paste wax; buff gently to replenish wood with oil and to restore luster. Oak runners should be treated in the same manner. Metal strips can be rubbed with steel wool, finished with a coat of mineral oil.

SHAKER PANTRY BOXES *(top right)*, typically stained red, yellow, or blue-green, were colored with vegetable dyes, the basis of which was clay, a natural preservative. Non-Shaker coopers also produced boxes, which can be mistaken for those made by the Shakers. To preserve vegetable-dyed boxes, keep them dust-free and avoid extremes in temperature, particularly strong heat from sunlight.

APOTHECARY CHEST *(bottom right)* had been painted gray to match other storage units in a 19th-century chemist's shop. The collector who found it was able to discern flecks of original red paint underneath and had the chest professionally restored. Its current care is gentle dusting in a climate-controlled environment.

PRESERVING PAINTED WOODS

Woodenware from the 17th and 18th centuries was either left in its natural grain or decorated with paint. Treen, a term applied to commonly used objects made from trees, is sought by collectors who attempt to find old pieces in well-preserved condition, particularly with vestiges of original paint. Treen with painted motifs, floral patterns, or solid coats of red, gray, brown, green, and blue paint are considered especially desirable.

Painted motifs often included names stenciled by the firms that mass-produced them. Therefore, painted decoration may well serve as a historical reference. Good examples of late 19th-century decorated sleds are in the collection of Emery Goff and Bill Carhart of the Old Barn Annex in Brunswick, Maine. As sled connoisseurs, they are able to point out distinctive marks that are helpful to other collectors with a similar affinity. Antique boys' sleds, for instance, had tubular steel runners mounted on a solid piece of wood which was often painted and signed by the owner. Boys' sleds that have survived the wear and tear of "belly-flopping" may have middle portions with paint rubbed off. Girls' sleds, characterized by thin bentwood runners and delicate features, were often pushed from behind. Therefore, a girl's sled with scuff marks bears a sign of its past history.

While some collectors choose to preserve the weathered quality of time-worn woods, others may elect to have paint restored to a more pristine condition. If you prefer the latter, rely on the expertise of a professional paint restorer.

CARING FOR WEATHERED WOODS

Rugged wood furniture can be relegated to the outdoors providing the climate is temperate. Texas collector Beverly Jacomini points to her country table and chairs as living proof. "I don't spoil them at all," she says. "Every once in a while I'll clean them with soap and then wax with a bit of paste wax." Sheltered by the porch where they stay all year, the table and chairs maintain a weathered patina. Sturdy by nature and originally intended for the outdoors, the old Texas table has a two-board pine top with pecan wood legs.

OVERSIZED TABLE *(left)* **and early American flatback chairs are brought inside periodically to escape the elements.**

OLD PLANK TABLE *(below)* **with turn-of-the-century rush-seat chairs is transported outdoors for summer, stationed in a log cabin all winter.**

HORSE'S HEAD WEATHER VANE is a 19th-century design molded of copper. After years of exposure to the elements, this has oxidized to a light green shade. The patina is an honest sign of aging and authenticity.

THE WEAR AND CARE OF METALS

It is unlikely that metal objects will warp or crack; however, they are subject to tarnish and corrosion. Old pieces such as weather vanes and sleds that have been exposed to the ravages of outdoor life will have varying degrees of tarnish. Many collectors choose not to rub off signs of age, preferring instead to leave a greened patina on copper, a browned antiqueness on metal.

Extreme tarnishing results in corrosion, a rough, scaly texture notable for crevices and deformities.

Of all the metals, iron and tin are considered the most susceptible to corrosion. Since both of these materials were used in the manufacture of weather vanes and sleds, it stands to reason that these old favorites will be tinged with age— a desirable state in the view of many collectors.

SWAN'S HEAD SLED (above) owned by Emery Goff and Bill Carhart dates back to the late 1800s. Its ornamented steel runners bear evidence of corrosion, a process that will continue if the piece is left outdoors or in a moist environment.

While discoloration and roughness are acceptable, if not desirable conditions, corrosion that is allowed to run rampant may ultimately destroy an object. To halt the erosive process, keep metal pieces indoors and free of moisture.

Rust is another attacker of metal, particularly ironwork. Rusted iron, if not controlled, will eventually corrode to a powdery substance, so it is advisable to curb the rusting process on antique ornaments. A suggested remedy is to dip the item in kerosene, then rub with fine steel wool. When the kerosene is dry, the piece can be oiled or painted according to preference.

85

CARING FOR OLD CLOTH

Collectors and curators of antique textiles agree that a beneficent environment is a temperate room with low humidity (fabrics absorb moisture) and low-voltage lighting. Sunlight, or even snow reflection, is a notorious enemy of fabrics, since direct light causes fading and deterioration of fibers. Another hazard is storing valuable textiles in trunks or sealing them in airtight containers such as glass enclosures. If you choose to display collections under glass, as in the shadow-box arrangements shown here, the enclosure must not be airtight or fabrics will eventually disintegrate. Folding fabrics for long periods of time is also to be avoided, for fear of causing creases and cracks. For the short intervals that fabrics may be folded, it is recommended that lengths of wadded acid-free tissue paper be inserted in the folds for protection and that fabrics be refolded at regular intervals. Rolling, rather than folding, is the more desirable method of storing hangings such as rugs or quilts.

Since most old textiles were woven or knitted from natural fibers—that is, cotton, wool, linen, or silk—each has individual needs regarding cleaning. However, dry cleaning is *not* safe for any antique fabric. Hand-washing in lukewarm water with a mild detergent is considered proper care for most fabrics, but since many antique dyes are not colorfast, it is advisable to consult a professional restorer before cleaning an antique textile. Moreover, to assure a fabric's longevity, dust it occasionally and guard against stains and spills.

DOLLS' CLOTHES AND MEMORABILIA *(above)* are contained in shadow boxes, mounted on taffeta with dressmaker pins. The boxes are fitted with sliding glass lids to allow air in and to facilitate dusting.

COLLECTION OF SMALL TEXTILES *(left),* hung in a hallway, is safe from direct light, excess dryness, or moisture.

HOMESPUN CHILDREN'S CLOTHES *(right)* are rotated often, rolled and covered with cotton sheets when stored. They are aired outdoors and hand-washed periodically.

THE LURE OF DECOYS

Good form and old paint are the characteristics that attract collectors to decoys of all species. Of the two, form is the more important factor, as no amount of paint will camouflage poor proportions.

Old working decoys are likely to be weather-beaten and lacking in paint—signs of prior service as hunting devices, and hardly objectionable conditions where most collectors are concerned. Water stains, for example, commonly found on floating decoys, do not diminish a good decoy's value to its owner. Rather, the marks indicate history to Dr. George Starr, whose collection of old decoys numbers about 1,600. To preserve his flock, Dr. Starr washes the wood carvings annually with soap and water, then rubs them with a little lemon oil.

Newer breeds of decoys, carved by Sherman Hensal, also attract collectors in search of good form and color. This craftsman employs exterior enamel and marine varnish to give his birds long-lasting finishes; he recommends a reasonable amount of humidity to prevent paint from cracking.

OLD FLOATING DECOY *(right)* is an eider duck with a mussel in its mouth. An example of good form and well-aged wood, this bird receives a yearly bath and oil rub. The seam around its neck indicates a decoy whose head was carved separately, then attached to the body.

NEW DUCK *(far right)*, decorative carving by Sherman Hensal, lays no claim to being a hunter's lure.

A GOOD CLIMATE FOR TOYS

The home gallery devoted to Bernard Barenholtz's extensive toy collection is climate-controlled at a temperature of 70 degrees with 45-percent humidity. Apart from an occasional dusting, the owner gives no special treatment to his old wooden "horse cycles," as his children call them.

Climate is considered the prime factor in a collector's care of valuable old toys. High humidity can cause cast iron to rust, paint to flake, nickel to pit, and tin to mold. The most efficient method of controlling humidity and protecting toys from its harmful effects is with a dehumidifier. Other means of absorbing moisture are boxes of baking soda and bags of silica gel.

If you have toys with layer upon layer of dirt, a mild soap and water solution may vastly improve their condition. To remove dirt from paint or lithography, try a solution of one part baking soda to five parts water or a mild dishwashing detergent. Strong cleansers should be avoided as they may damage or fade old paint. A light coating of oil or liquid wax should be applied after cleaning—a step that will protect and enhance the finish for years.

Broken toys, particularly if they are rare, should be professionally restored.

ANTIQUE HORSE TOYS, from the early 1900s, were made for children. Now in the hands of adult collectors, these hobbyhorses are treated with tender loving care, protected from extremes in temperature, dusted and polished occasionally.

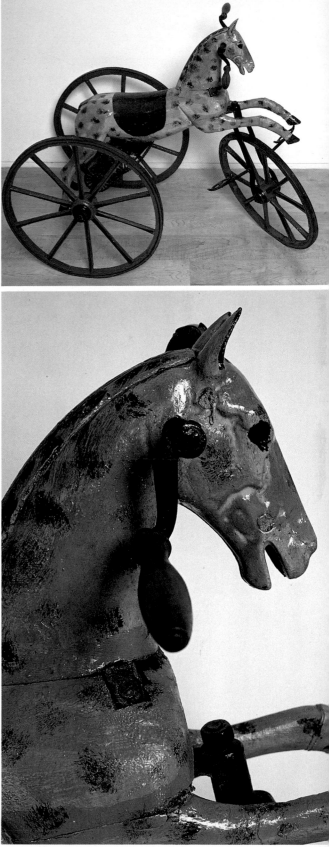

91

SPECIAL CARE FOR MECHANICAL TOYS

Toys with movable parts are subject to breakdown more often than stationary models and are the most difficult to repair because of their intricate workings. Considering the years of handling that old toys have been exposed to, it's a triumph to find mechanical types in perfect condition. Serious breaks do diminish a toy's value in the collectors' marketplace, but there are skilled professionals equipped to mend defects.

Among the most fragile varieties are 19th-century squeak toys made of chalk or papier-mâché. Collector Pete Riffle protects his from cracking by controlling moisture with a dehumidifier, keeping an even temperature, and enclosing the squeak toys in a glass cabinet. He shuns any kind of repair work because of the delicate materials of the toys

and advises other collectors to refrain from touching up the paint or gluing any of the parts together. He even suggests using restraint when it comes to dusting!

Whirligigs, pull toys, and mechanical banks are valued for their animated character as well as for their overall condition. These painted toys, whether wood or cast iron, require the same care as any valued antique, specifically climate control and gentle dusting (a feather duster is

SQUEAK TOY *(far left)* made of papier-mâché is mounted on a wooden base with paper bellows. This late 1800s antique is fragile by nature and must be protected from extremes in temperature as well as excess humidity. Pennsylvania Dutch toys such as this were made of either papier-mâché or chalk, fragile materials that are prone to cracks and splits. Its owner, Pete Riffle, keeps it enclosed in a glass cabinet, where the toy receives a minimal amount of handling save for an occasional dusting.

MECHANICAL BANKS *(above left)* are kept in good working order for enjoyment. These cast-iron toys usually have a trap underneath which releases money. Repairing a broken trap is an easy matter for a skilled restorer and will not decrease the bank's value.

WOODEN WHIRLIGIGS *(left)* are from the turn of the century, found in Southern Illinois. They are in original condition with working parts in order. Forms of entertainment as well as decoration, they are protected from excess moisture and extremes in temperature so that the wood will not swell or the paint chip.

PULL TOY *(right)* is carved and painted wood, from the early 1900s. When the bottom weight is pulled, the cat's tail goes down and its head rises. The toy, in good working condition, is a source of amusement that requires little care. This is mounted high on a wall so that it can be easily activated and observed as a piece of folk art.

suggested). Since they are playful by nature, a hands-off policy would run contrary to their purpose; they are most enjoyable when in motion.

Mechanical toys in fragile condition may be put on a high shelf where their winsome qualities, rather than their working parts, can be admired from a distance. Since old mechanical toys represent increasingly valuable collectors' items, they should all be handled with due respect, no matter what their condition.

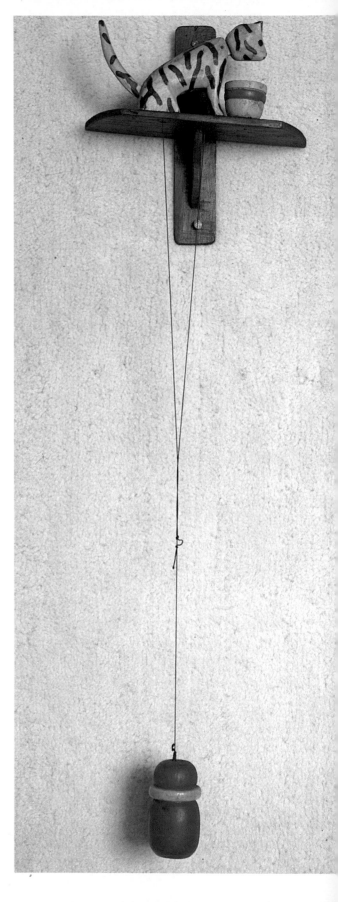

STUFFED ANIMALS

Many an old Teddy bear displays signs of the aftereffects of having been poked in the eye, chewed on the ear, pinched on the nose, or carried by the arm. Those loyal bears (and other pets) who've survived decades of loving abuse can live on to even riper old age if you treat them to some special care prescribed by collectors Kate and Joel Kopp.

First of all, there is no condition that could be labeled unbearable. That goes for bald spots, amputated limbs, displaced stuffing. An old bear, no matter how impaired, evokes love, not pity—and craves attention. If yours has split its seams, sew the rip together with thread (old, if possible) that matches the fur, making sure to replace any stuffing that may have leaked out. Enter the fur from the wrong side and exit through the right side with a lacing stitch. And if your bear is emaciated from lack of stuffing, straw or excelsior can be grafted from other animals. Alternatives to antique stuffing are scraps of stockings or clean panty hose without elastic. Sagging bears should be gently stuffed, using the blunt end of a crochet hook or the eraser on the end of a pencil. Be careful not to overstuff the bear, so as not to strain the aging fur.

Vacuuming old bears will keep them free of dust, but extremely dirty bears may need a bath. The procedure: cover a table with a towel, then fill a small pan with warm water and about one-eighth cupful mild liquid detergent. Using a long-handled, soft-bristled brush, dip it into the solution and shake off excess moisture. Starting with the head

(removing stickpin eyes if it has them), brush on suds with clockwise strokes, rinsing the brush with clean water between applications. Wipe off the lightly soaped bear with a damp washcloth in a clockwise motion. As dirt is removed, rinse the cloth before reapplying. Then, being careful not to disturb stitching on nose and mouth, brush on a final rinse of warm water to which a small amount of fabric softener has been added. Do not allow the animal to get soaked during any step. After washing the head, work on the torso and limbs, avoiding felt paws and digit stitching. Wrap the bear in a towel, and comb gently, beginning with the head. A fine-tooth pet comb works well on facial fur, while wide-spaced teeth are best for fluffing up matted fur. The damp bear can be dried on a clothesline, suspended by nylon fishing line tied loosely around its waist (not neck).

A word about newfound old bears whose habitat may have been an attic or basement: their fur could be a breeding ground for local parasites, so a body check is advisable before engaging in bear hugs. If the animal is suspect, confine it to an isolation box with a stick of insecticide for a day. The guests will not survive.

BUNNY IN CALICO DRESS (left) is stuffed with straw and presumed to be from about 1915. It usually resides in an Easter basket, protected from additional wear and tear.

VESTED BEAR (right), minus an ear and nose, shows signs of being loved to death. An early 19th-century toy, it's dressed in homespun clothes, but otherwise left in its tattered state.

THE CARE AND FEEDING OF BASKETS

Because they are woven from organic materials, baskets need to be cleaned and fed in order to maintain their suppleness. Antiques dealer Paul Madden sponges his old Nantucket baskets with a small amount of mild detergent and water. Feeding consists of a fine spray of light furniture oil "every few years." While the application of oil will darken the patina, this look of age is very desirable. Another expert—a collector of American Indian baskets—recommends regular sponging with a solution of 40 percent castor oil, 60 percent alcohol, then wiping off the excess with a soft cloth.

Deterrents to the aging process, and, in fact, major threats to a basket's life, are bugs, specifically powder-post beetles. Madden warns, "If you see any tiny holes or if you shake the basket and a fine powder falls out, this usually means bugs." His remedy: place sick basket in a large garbage bag with a towel inside (to absorb chemicals) and douse with garden spray. Leave closed for 24 hours.

Restorers Sue and Neil Connell advise that misshapen baskets can be restored to their original shape after a soaking in water, and drying with supports. When repair is necessary, they use old splint and reed in closely matched tones, soak them until pliable, and reweave the damaged area.

OLD BASKETS grow darker with age, the application of oil, and exposure to sunlight—all of which enhance their patina. Misting with water wards off dust and brittleness.

SHELLWORK

Wooden whatnot boxes and picture frames encrusted with shells—the handwork of mid-19th-century seafarers who whiled away their time making gifts for their sweethearts—have come to be known as sailors' valentines. In the category of hobo or tramp art, this early shellwork has gained importance as a found-object form of Americana.

Two connoisseurs of shellwork, Don Kelly and Warren Fitzsimmons, display their collection in their jointly owned Captain Jefferds Inn, Kennebunkport, Maine. They claim all of the shellwork, including commercially made trinket boxes constructed of cardboard and covered with seashells, is extremely fragile and subject to broken or missing shells. The owners rely on an old-fashioned feather duster for gentle, routine care, so as not to shake loose precarious shells. If loosening does occur, they recommend using a good epoxy glue to reattach missing shells. However, Kelly eschews "patch jobs," claiming he'd rather leave a piece in the condition he bought it in.

Vacuuming is another recommended means of caring for shellwork, providing the suction is not too strong. Scrubbing shellwork is frowned upon, given its fragile nature.

SHELL BOXES, also known as sailors' valentines, were made by 19th-century seamen as tokens of affection.

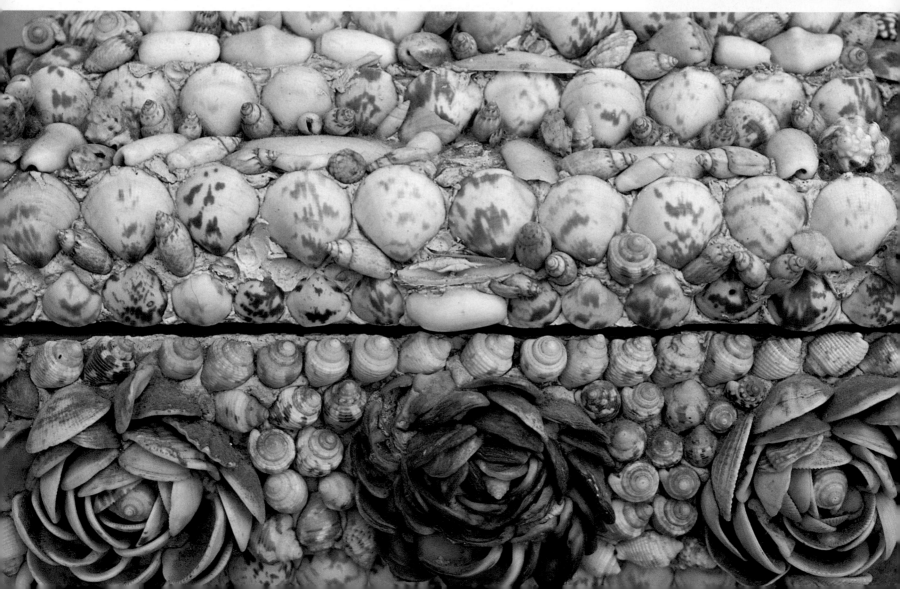

ABOUT HOOKED AND RAG RUGS

Basic rules for maintaining old hooked and rag rugs:

- Turn rugs frequently so they wear evenly
- Keep out of direct sunlight
- Always use with a pad to prevent slipping and preserve weave
- Roll when storing
- Vacuum regularly; never dry clean
- Repair immediately if ends fray or weave begins to unravel
- If rug is fragile, or very rare, mount as art on wall rather than place on floor

Since vigorous washing or dry cleaning shortens old rugs' life span, regular vacuuming and airing are recommended for routine care.

A novel way of cleaning (and airing) was invented by Helene von Rosenstiel, a restorer who refreshes rag and hooked rugs by laying them on top of snow and tossing handfuls of snow on the rugs, then sweeping the snow off. This prevents rugs from getting too wet, she claims, and is an effective way of removing dust.

RAG RUGS *(below)*, from the late 1800s, illustrate braided round and woven rectangular types.

HOOKED RUG *(below)*, late 19th-century Connecticut, is in the Tree of Life motif.

FOLK ART CARE INDOORS AND OUT

Certain examples of rural folk art have survived years of outdoor exposure, such as shop signs, weather forecasters on tops of barns, and wind toys perched on fences. Many of these artifacts are now sheltered in the homes of collectors who treat them with the same respect accorded priceless heirlooms. However, some pieces are simply too massive or too heavy to consider bringing indoors. Hex signs, originally placed on barn gables, belong to the outdoors with nature as their guardian. Where weather vanes are concerned, however, the most favorable environment may well be the indoors. Antique vanes, particularly the hollow three-dimensional figures of hammered copper handmade before 1850, should surely be brought indoors for safekeeping against thievery.

If you're uncertain as to the date or authenticity of a weather vane, "find yourself a good dealer," suggests one collector, who claims, "Fakes are very hard to spot. However, repairs made on old weather vanes tend to be obvious; soldering and repainting can be detected under a black light." Whether or not a repair diminishes the value of a vane depends on the nature of the restoration and the rarity of the piece.

Outdoor materials, typically copper, brass, and tin, are subject to tarnish or corrosion even when they are brought inside. Although the old patina often adds to an object's antique charm, keeping metals in a dry place inhibits excess corrosion. When metals are subjected to dampness, a light coating of vegetable oil applied once a year is recommended.

STONE BUST *(below)* was purchased by Betty Barenholtz, who cites its origin as Medina, Ohio. It has lived outside for nearly ten years on a granite slab, withstanding the elements as well as any other threats to safety.

HEX SIGN *(left)* was salvaged from a Pennsylvania Dutch barn in Brown County, Kansas. About a hundred years old, its vibrant colors are thought to be original. Jerry Smith, who bought the sign twenty years ago, marvels at its fine condition and sees no reason to tamper with it. "They had much better paint in those days," he says, referring to the barely chipped finish. The 6-foot-square sign, once thought to ward off evil, contains louvers to enable air to circulate through the barn.

VICTORY WEATHER VANE *(above)* looks precisely as she did twelve years ago when purchased by Bernard Barenholtz from a dealer. Probably a late 1880s piece, she bears few signs of age. The owner, who enjoys her presence at the entrance of his home, has created a glass-walled indoor gallery for outdoor folk art, including a variety of large weather vanes.

HEART WEATHER VANE continues to endure the elements. Because of their increasing value, many old vanes are being brought inside for safekeeping. Unrestored old pieces are the most desirable.

A CLUSTER OF CANES *(above left)* is displayed in a stand where each shape can be appreciated for its distinct personality. The sectioned stand holds each one upright so that the carved handles can be clearly seen; touching is permitted but not encouraged. These 19th-century walking sticks include subjects favored among folk artists, such as a woman's leg, sinuous snakes, and primitive heads.

CARVED-FISH CANE *(below left)*, made from one piece of wood, stands alone as a piece of sculpture. Probably early 19th century, the cane appears as it did when it was purchased by a collector of American folk art, who recommends buying canes only in good condition.

CARVED-HAND CANES *(above right)* were favorite subjects of 19th-century folk artists, who used whalebone as well as wood to create fists of diverse proportions.

LIZARD AND CROCODILE STICKS *(below right)* carved from tree branches were popular turn-of-the-century motifs. These sturdy pieces bear no signs of restoration.

CARE EXTENDED TO CANES

Like all wood carvings, old canes are valued for their craftsmanship. Three P's determine a cane's desirability: patina, proportion, and personality. These qualities attract the connoisseur whose goal is to find a walking stick in fine condition and to keep it that way with appropriate care.

The many canes that one Midwestern collector has acquired through the years have long been retired from active duty as walking sticks; they've been elevated to the level of folk art. He considers the hand-carved pieces forms of sculpture and cares for them with restraint. A gentle dusting is the only routine treatment they receive.

Since the shafts are generally narrow and worn down from use, vigorous polishing could prove to be destructive; therefore, hands off is the best policy. The same applies to canes' heads whose delicate carvings may be easily damaged. Humidifying a too-dry room is the maintenance program collectors find most satisfactory.

PRESERVING SIGNS OF EARLY AMERICANA

Advertising trade signs were exposed to wind-lashings and downpours as they hung outside of shops, conveying graphic messages to passersby who could neither read nor write. Many of these turn-of-the-century signs have found shelter in collectors' homes and antiques shops, for they are considered valuable forms of Americana, especially if they are in respectable condition.

How to maintain or improve the condition of old signs depends on the material from which they were made. According to one knowledgeable collector, Jerry Smith—whose trade signs number about 100—the earliest material was a slab of wood, followed by tin, porcelain, wrought iron, bronze, and brass. To preserve wood signs, he uses a product called Finish Feeder, which restores oils to weather-beaten woods. Old tin, the most perishable of sign materials, tends to shed paint, a condition that Smith has "never found a cure for." He cautions against using varnish to make paint hold, claiming "it just doesn't work." His routine care includes wiping metal signs with Sanil wax, which contains a cleaning agent and protects painted or lithographed surfaces. Porcelain, which Smith

refers to as "pretty tough stuff," can also be cleaned with Sanil wax and rubbed with fine steel wool if it has any areas of rust. His treatment of wrought-iron signs is similar to that of porcelain; occasionally he will improve the patina of a black iron piece by wiping a thin solution of flat black paint on the surface, then wiping it off immediately, so the improvement is very subtle. Brass and bronze, the sturdiest of all materials,

respond to dusting and polishing.

As for the day-to-day climate for old advertising signs that now reside indoors, a moderate temperature should be maintained.

TRADE SIGNS *(above)* **from the late 1800s and early 1900s all appear in their original condition, preserved in a humidity-controlled room. They include barber poles and optician and locksmith signs.**

PIGS FOR SALE is a primitive sign with words as well as symbol.

107

Ways to Display

How to live with what you can't live without? Here are **ideas for displaying many collections,** *including where to find an appropriate place in your home,* **how to arrange, mount, and illuminate** *specific objects, types of lighting to use, and directions for hanging quilts and other textiles.*

If you're among the estimated one-third of the American population who amass some set of objects with an obvious degree of seriousness, your passion may lead to a common dilemma. How to live with what you collect? And even if you consider collecting a private pursuit of happiness, displaying the fruits of your search may add to your enjoyment.

Perhaps you choose to live in the midst of your collections with favorite things always at arm's reach, or you may be the kind of collector who is intent upon maintaining order and vigilant about cleaning. Displaying then becomes a question of editing and careful placement.

How you display collections is a personal matter, after all, and these real-life examples are intended to inspire you to reevaluate what you own and to display it where it suits you best. In the process of choosing an appropriate place for objects, you'll also want to consider the effect of the display, its overall impact in the context of a room.

SEVERAL GENERATIONS OF TEDDY BEARS *(preceding pages)* **gather outside a collector's house. These descendants of the famed Teddy are usually given pride of place in a toy-filled room.**

OLD NEW ENGLAND BASKETS *(far left)* **make use of a deep window recess as if it were a shadow box.**

SOUTHERN POTTERY PITCHERS *(left),* **1840–1930, dot the sill of a picture window close to nested rye-straw baskets and a Tennessee iron weather vane, c. 1880.**

111

WHERE TO DISPLAY

The kitchen is an obvious place for displaying utilitarian objects that hark back to colonial days when cooking tools were stationed by the hearth. Hands-on collections such as ironware, pottery, or baskets can be exhibited in their natural environment—in the kitchen, dining area, or keeping room—hooked to peg racks, perched on shelves, or even suspended from the ceiling.

DRIED HERBS hang from an antique bed mat *(right)* suspended from the ceiling of a traditional keeping room. The mat is the kind used between mattress and rope strings on an early bed.

OLD IRON, BRASS, AND COPPER TOOLS *(below)* dangle from a primitive wood rack, readily available for daily use, decorative when unemployed.

HERBAL WREATHS, DRIED FLOWERS, AND HEARTS *(right)* are artfully hung from the ceiling beam and on the paneled wall over a brick fireplace. The simple wood mantel serves as a shelf for 19th-century maple-sugar molds from New Hampshire. Hooked rug and cut-paper valentine contribute to the tableau of country objects.

PEG RACK *(below),* a shelved version of the Shaker type, holds a parade of 19th-century cast-iron toys. And next to old tin lanterns and a brass horn is a display of miniatures on shelves scaled to match their dimensions. This kind of wall unit can provide a nesting place for many different collections that you may want to integrate into a public room.

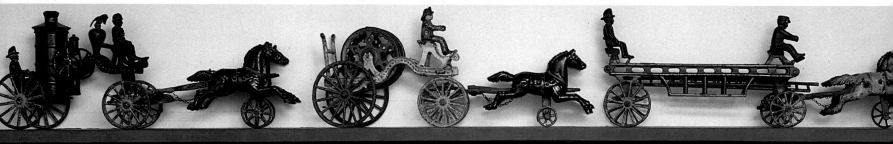

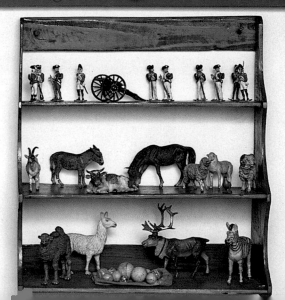

Walls, by virtue of their flat, open planes, are receptive to a display of collectibles. Take a cue from the Shakers who discovered that simple wooden peg racks would keep objects at eye level on the outer limits of a room, thus creating order among worldly possessions.

PEWTER, COPPER, AND IRON *(above)* indicate a cook's preference for tools of yesteryear. Within arm's reach are trivets and long-handled implements hung from a strip of molding over which 19th-century pewter shines forth.

CARVED APPLES *(right)* stand on a pine shelf unit built expressly for them. These popular flea market finds are old and new varieties, some of which conceal miniature toys inside hollow cores.

A quick survey of empty spaces in your home may turn up nooks and corners for displaying collections. Above doorways, for instance. Or a naked corner somewhere. What about an exposed side of a wooden cupboard? Stair landings can be the stage for a gathering of rag dolls, as can an antique bench or blanket chest. After you've focused on forgotten spaces, take a new look at the candidates for display. If you plan to nail things up, try a layout on the floor first. Or, if you're simply placing a few well-chosen things in an empty niche, experiment with abandon.

ANTIQUE FOOD CHOPPERS *(above)* appear to be tossed over a doorway, scattered on blank white space.

ANTIQUE STUFFED DOLLS *(right)*, dating back to 1915, huddle on an out-of-the-way shelf.

OLD IRON SCISSORS *(far left)* cut interesting figures when hung on the side of a cupboard, blades open.

SOUTHERN STONEWARE CROCKS AND JARS *(left)* fill an unused corner with character. Missing lids can be replaced with wooden rounds, cut to fit and stained. Topless jugs become vases when filled with fragrant eucalyptus leaves.

WEATHERED BIRDHOUSES AND NESTS *(below),* collected in the New Hampshire countryside, have a sanctuary of their own in one remote corner of a kitchen—complete with dried branches.

FINDING A PLACE FOR YOUR COLLECTION

Where to display a collection depends upon what space you find convenient and appropriate for the number of pieces you find presentable. That space may not be immediately apparent, that is, until you take a new survey of each room, peek into corners, prowl hallways and staircases.

Unexpected places for display may turn up in the search, particularly if you take stock of your collections first. Suppose you've amassed rag dolls since childhood, only to park them in an attic trunk. Seize the opportunity to show them off, clustered together on a staircase landing or antique chair. The same applies to Teddy bears that may have been retired to a closet when the children gave up toys for a stereo set.

If your collection is fragile—miniature dolls, historic glass flasks, or rare pottery, for instance—protect the pieces in a recessed shelf or a remote cupboard where they can be seen but not harmed.

Feel free to experiment. To open new territories where favorite things can be viewed is a challenge. The unique settings shown here were orchestrated by adventurous collectors with a keen eye for scale and the reuse of space.

HANGING RACK (left), stained the same tone as woodwork, holds Americana pewter, framed by colonial windows. Plates and tankards are arranged by size. Taller pieces fill the space between shelf and chest. A tiny jug is hooked under the shelf.

NARROW RACK behind a kitchen door is an unlikely place for pottery and pewter. This surprise element is a welcome sight from all angles of the room, since the door is shut most of the time.

HALL OF ART gives purpose to an otherwise ordinary narrow space. Both sides are nearly covered with folk images, including reverse paintings and theorems.

PARALLEL CEILING RODS support herbs and flowers that dry in colorful rows. This indoor bower also contains a collector's handiwork: wreaths and arrangements made from an assortment of natural materials on display all year.

CORNER OF A WHITE-TILED BATHROOM COUNTER provides a prescribed place for old medicine bottles. These flea market finds are appealing in their color and size variations, and their similar identity.

HUMBLE STAIRCASE is turned into a folk art gallery with Pennsylvania German-inspired theorems, by contemporary artist David Ellinger. Arriving at such a well-balanced scheme requires an initial layout on the floor. The background here is a subtle design that harmonizes with stenciled art.

FOLK MINIATURES *(right)* border a primitive oil painting of a child. Naïve wall motifs, painted with old tin stencils, are in keeping with the small folk objects on display.

BEAR MEMORABILIA *(far right)*, including Royal Doulton china, pewter molds, and pottery mugs, are encased on a shelf, shadow-box fashion. A small rack elevates some of the collection; such units are useful display surfaces on which to arrange diminutive items.

OLD BOOTMAKERS' SIGNS *(below)* once stood for 17th- and 18th-century trade. Now they stand in a collector's window silhouetted against a distant landscape of hill country.

AN OVERFLOW OF DECOYS led to the construction of this poolroom, where hundreds of carved wood species, retired from hunting, sit on shelves designed for them. This aquatic museum is also a watering place for houseguests.

HOW TO DISPLAY

Just as there are no set rules on *where* to display, there are no absolutes on *how*. But we've culled some guidelines that are applicable to many situations. First, decide what it is you want to display and where it will be most appreciated. Think of the collection as a graphic composition, somewhat like a store-window display that has a focal point with a complementary background. Perhaps one piece, such as a sculptural weather vane or decoy, demands a discrete place. On the other hand, some small pieces such as scrimshaw or baskets gain impact from the company of their fellows. In this case, groups are more emphatic. Another consideration is how the

BEARS IN BASKETS WITH HOMESPUN FABRICS *(above)* are brought together in a pleasing display. One towel rack balanced on a strip of pegs is a repository for layers of checkered and fringed cloth from colonial days. Prized Teddy bears sit in old baskets, one cub pinned to a panel of homespun cotton. Stenciling *(right)* frames the scheme, which includes a lineup of small baskets hung on pegs and illuminated by a pottery lamp.

display looks from various angles. View it from different vantage points, shifting pieces until the arrangement appeals to you.

SPACE

Space is a factor both within and around a collection. Baskets hung together from a ceiling are visually appealing in their overall texture; however, a cluster of pots needs some margins to emphasize varied shapes.

GRANITEWARE *(below)* is compatible with a 1930s stove whose top shelf displays an old scale, a corn muffin mold, and teakettles. A wall rack holds a wire basket, ladles, pots and pans, and other cookware.

NEW ENGLAND AND PENNSYLVANIA BASKETS *(right)* are massed on a kitchen ceiling where they can be reached for daily use or viewed overhead.

A display of quilts, rugs, and coverlets serves as an artistic statement, a raison d'être beyond the mere pride of ownership. And the avenues for display increase with every spare inch of space.

Expanses of white wall are likely areas on which to mount an important quilt or large-scale rug, remembering that ample margins around the piece emphasize its pattern and texture. Just as an imposing painting requires generous viewing room, a bold textile demands open space around it.

Smaller items—doll quilts or textile fragments—are less demanding; they can be hung as a group on wall spaces, as you would compose a series of pictures.

While aesthetics may be the point of a display, there is also a practical aspect: preserving the condition of the pieces you're showing. Textiles, in fact, should be rotated and periodically rested (see Chapter 3, page 87).

When you've designated which pieces will hang where, follow the procedure of knowledgeable collectors who are careful to protect their collectibles when readying them for display (see "How to Hang a Quilt," page 151).

TURN-OF-THE-CENTURY QUILTS draped over a balcony railing make a strong decorative impact on the sitting room below. Unified by color and geometric pattern, they provide a light background for a stable of rocking horses, c. 1900. Quilts include a "Double Wish Chain" from Ohio, second from left, and a "Feathered Star" from St. Louis, third from left. Others are from Southern Illinois.

Incidentally, quilts and coverlets needn't be spread out to be displayed effectively. They can be folded in an open cupboard, confined to one economical area where their diverse patterns will intermingle.

HOMESPUN BLANKETS AND COVERLETS *(above)* **are carefully folded in a step-back cupboard; here the patchwork of pattern is displayed in confined quarters.**

AMISH QUILTS *(above left),* **mounted on specially designed panels, have the impact of contemporary paintings. Their patterns: "Nine Patch," left, and "Diamonds," right.**

ANTIQUE AND NEW NAVAJO RUGS *(left)* **fill walls with intense color and Southwestern culture.**

DOLL QUILTS *(far left),* **from the 19th and 20th centuries, are hung like pictures, their geometric patterns relating to one another. T-shaped quilts were made for four-poster beds.**

ANTIQUE WASHBOARDS *(right)* from New England, 1850–1910, find an appropriate place on a laundry room wall. Ranging from miniature to full size, they form a composition of related shapes and corrugated textures. White space is evenly distributed to allow each one ample visibility.

FIRKINS AND PANTRY BOXES *(center top),* the earliest dated 1796, are stacked on the floor and table of this skylit room. White curtain and whitewashed floor emphasize the subtleties of their shades, including a rare pink pigment.

PAINTED CUPBOARD *(center bottom),* native to New York State, is an ideal showcase for sets of blue-and-white spongeware. Larger bowls and pitchers are accommodated on top where they are safe but highly visible. The door can be closed to protect contents.

STOCKING STRETCHERS *(far right)* distinguish another wall in the laundry room shown at left. This collection, originally from New England and Pennsylvania, fills several feet of white space with elongated wooden forms. A copper bowl and pans hang from the back of a beam, a decoy sits on top.

BEAR FAMILY *(left),* dressed in homespun clothes, convenes at a table suited to its size.

ORDINARY CLOSET *(right)* becomes an uncommon display area for antique quilts when the door is propped open with a Southern pottery crock filled with walking sticks.

PATCHWORK QUILT *(far right)* in "Robbing Peter to Pay Paul" pattern is a vivid background for a painted chest, c. 1860. This shadow-box type of display makes use of an odd niche where stoneware, baskets, and tin animals are sheltered.

KEY BASKET *(below),* designed as a wall receptacle for keys, is reused as a door display for dried flowers.

OLD GARDEN TOOL *(below right)* is put back into service as a display prop. Rake prongs, minus handle, provide a sectioned rack for bunches of drying herbs.

135

COLOR

Similarity of tone unifies a collection; contrasting colors dramatize it. For example, the blue-and-white spongeware housed in a blue cupboard (page 133) shows how colors coalesce, while the mix of redware and pewter (page 118) is enriched by bright blue walls and a red-painted rack. White, as shown here, acts as a dramatic backdrop for colors.

HEART-SHAPED MOLDS *(above)* **gain prominence on a white wall and distinction from the barn-red woodwork surrounding them.**

TIN COOKIE CUTTERS *(left),* **mounted on cutting boards, and a large group of wood molds, similarly toned, are clearly defined on a white wall.**

OLD IRON TRIVETS *(right)* **become even bolder when hung against a white background with a wide molding of earth-toned wood.**

There are two ways to view a collection: one, for its overall impact —an impression that conveys its owner's affection and years of tracking down related objects; two, for the distinctive character of each piece, such as color, texture, or shape.

SPLINT BASKETS *(right),* hung flat against the wall on centered nails, become shadow boxes for stuffed toys. Cats, made of printed fabric, which was cut out, then stuffed, were as popular at the turn of the century as they are now.

FOLK ART FIGURES AND OLD STONEWARE *(center)* have a fitting home in a barn-red wall niche with white shelves. Rocking horse and pig by artist Larry Koosed.

TREEN *(top far right)* is a monochromatic display on a 19th-century spoon rack with original paint.

RED RAG BALLS *(bottom far right),* newly made, accent the subdued colors of an old braided rug underneath.

STICK-UP DECOYS *(below),* cut from tin and painted to mimic shorebirds, are clamped to wide-planked walls painted in an early American ocher color.

139

ILLUMINATION

How much and what kind are the key questions to ask when lighting a collection. As a general rule, the source of light, natural or artificial, should contribute as little heat as possible. Since vegetable dyes, writing inks, and watercolors are subject to fading, light on painted surfaces should be minimized.

Sunlight, a potential danger to antique materials, can be controlled by shades or redirected by louvers. Ultraviolet-absorbing plastic can be placed over windows to further reduce the flood of light.

Another way to guard against harmful effects is to rotate objects seasonally and to use dimmer switches for control over the amount of artificial light focused on your display.

DISPLAY LIGHTING

Incandescent lights, such as spots and floods, shed a smooth beam of light on specific subjects. Floodlights "wash" an area, while spotlights focus on one spot. Because this type of lighting can fade or burn textiles and other vulnerable materials, low-voltage varieties are recommended. Spots and floods can be mounted on a ceiling track.

Mounted directly over subjects, these lights provide "down-lighting." Stationed on the floor, spots and floods provide "up-lighting," which dramatizes a silhouette.

Fluorescent lights deliver more illumination with less damaging heat. The most common forms used for display purposes are strips, or light boxes, that can be mounted on the underside of shelf units or inside cupboards.

ROCKINGHAM POTTERY AND SPONGEWARE *(below)* **are showcased in custom-built display boxes with recessed fluorescent lighting. Glass doors protect against dust and breakage, but permit ready access when pieces are to be used.**

OLD TIN GRATERS *(above)* are converted to lanterns with the simple addition of votive candles. They exemplify American Country lighting in its most basic form. Since the material is tin, it can withstand the constant low heat of the candles.

ANTIQUE SHOE RACK *(right),* rescued from a shoe factory, is recycled as a floating shelf unit for country pieces. Natural back-lighting from the window points up the color and form of old pottery and new glass storage jars.

SHAKER BOXES *(far right),* in a cupboard with other wood pieces, are illuminated by a nearby window. The tab curtains can be drawn to protect painted finishes from strong light.

WEATHER VANES are bathed in pools of light from track-mounted spots.

INSTALLATION

When considering where to display a collection, first imagine how it can be installed. Is it to have permanence or mobility, easy access or remoteness? Textiles, for instance, need to be rested periodically for their protection, so they are best hung from a freestanding rack or a Shaker-inspired peg rack—from which they can easily be taken down.

ANTIQUE CHILDREN'S CLOTHES *(left),* on hangers, are suspended from a peg rack—an efficient device that makes the most of any space.

EMBROIDERED SHOW TOWELS *(right)* were placed over everyday towels in early 19th-century homes. This collection is displayed on a folding wooden rack; for special show, one towel is tacked to the door.

PEG RACK *(below)* holds a wardrobe of 19th-century bonnets.

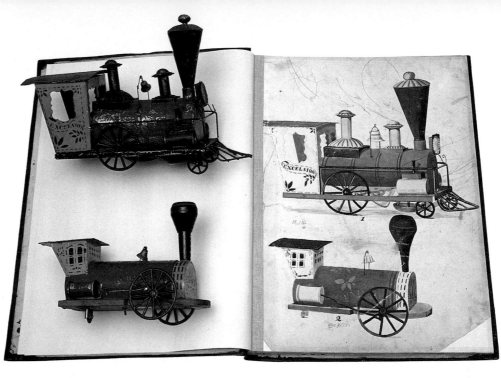

ANTIQUE QUILTS, HOMESPUN BLANKETS, AND CHILDREN'S WEAR *(left)* easily assimilate in a country bedroom. A wall-to-wall peg rack offers ample hanging space; a toy cart finds parking space on a chest.

TRIVETS AND MOLDS *(below)* obviously have a heart theme in common, a good enough reason to mount them together on a white wall in balanced rows.

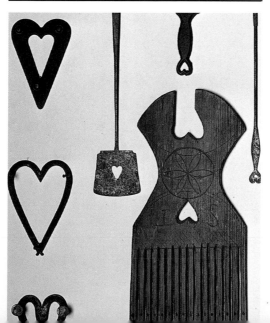

NINETEENTH-CENTURY TIN TOYS *(above)* are displayed on the pages of a sketchbook dated 1870, where original designs were executed.

The architecture of a room suggests ways in which collections can be installed. As an example, a period house with intimate rooms and low ceilings is receptive to strips of peg rack along tops of walls where antique clothes, hats, baskets, canes, and even Shaker or light child-size chairs could be spontaneously hung. Beamed ceilings are also ideal places to hang baskets attached by cup hooks or thin nails.

Built-in bookcases suit collections of pottery and miniatures, which can be interspersed with books for an eclectic grouping. And books themselves offer "installation" opportunities. Designer George Burn found that an old sketchbook illustrating his antique tin toys in explicit detail was an appropriate resting place for them.

147

INN SIGN *(left),* dated 1813, welcomed coach travelers. These wood signs, often painted on both sides, were pictorial, because much of the public could not read. The architectural detail on top and finials are unusual.

The city apartment of graphic designer and race car devotee Richard Trask sports an 8-foot by 9-foot display of old cars, starting with the first cast-iron versions of the early 1900s. It was at the suggestion of his wife, Jean, that the folk art quality toys were housed on one free wall in the dining room where they create a mural effect, rich with color and racing-car chronology. More than 150 cars are arranged according to vintage, many with their original drivers. Narrow white shelves set off the cars' colors and take up minimal space in the room.

RACING CARS *(above),* ranging from an inch to over two feet, are lined up on shelves. Old racing games are interspersed among the cars, which function as sculpture as well as entertainment.

"They recall memories of days gone by, of fabrics worn many years ago," says Margaret Cavigga, a noted collector of quilts who describes them as "emotional and visual art forms that represent safety and security as well as beauty." Indeed, these qualities are to be considered when displaying quilts so that their beauty will remain secure.

And since many old quilts represent a valuable investment, appreciating steadily as they age, it pays to handle them with care. Their worth is based on fine hand stitchery, intricacy of pattern, and condition. Like the Amish quilts collected here, each one harbors a colorful piece of history.

AMISH CRIB QUILTS, 1880–1940, are from Ohio's Wayne and Holmes counties. Quilts at lower left and upper right are "Nine Patch," a common Ohio Amish pattern. Others, from left, are "Mosaic," "Railroad Crossing," and "Tumbling Blocks."

150

HOW TO HANG A QUILT

As an endangered species, old quilts should be treated kindly, not abused with pushpins, staples, or nails. Piercing the fabric is certain to cause damage, so suppress any urge to hang a valuable quilt on impulse. The proper mounting of a quilt is quite simple and has the approval of experts, so rely on these fundamental guidelines:

Hang your quilt in such a way that its weight will be evenly distributed on four sides. If you hang a quilt by its top alone, within six months it's likely to be permanently misshapen.

The method shown here, suggested by quilt expert Michael Kile of Kiracofe and Kile in San Francisco, satisfies the basic requirements for preserving your quilt.

What you need is ½-inch Velcro tape cut into strips, needle and thread, a staple gun, and—depending on the composition of your walls—an artist's canvas stretcher, cut to the size of your quilt. (Velcro can be purchased by the yard in a dry goods or department store, or by the spool; check under "Notions" or "Trimmings" in the Yellow Pages. Canvas stretchers, also known as frames, are available from art supply stores.)

● Lay the quilt on the floor and find the top edge. If the pattern doesn't have an obvious top, pick the straightest side and use that as the top.

● Cut Velcro into 6-inch strips. Starting with the top edge of the quilt, sew the strips to the back near the binding, using a whipstitch. Leaving 2 inches between each strip, sew Velcro all around the quilt.

● Measure the quilt along Velcro strips you have sewn down, so you can cut similar strips to apply to the wall.

● If your wall is Sheetrock, wood, or cinder block, do *not* staple Velcro directly onto it. Instead, use an artist's canvas stretcher or frame. Staple the Velcro to the frame, then hang it as you would a large painting, using toggle bolts or screws with expansion anchors.

● Hang the quilt by pressing the Velcro strips together.

If the backing on your quilt is fragile, such as silk or, from early days, linsey-woolsey, *do not* use the Velcro method to hang it. Instead, sew a backing of prewashed cotton to the existing backing of the quilt, leaving an overhang of 6 to 8 inches on all sides. Then, fold the overhang around a frame that has also been stretched with prewashed cotton fabric. Fasten the overhang to the back of the frame, as if you were stretching an artist's canvas. This is a much more complicated method, but it will protect a very old or fragile quilt from further damage.

Properly hung, a quilt should not lose its shape. But to be on the safe side, Michael Kile recommends taking it down every year or so, to let the fabric rest. Fold the quilt and put it away; hang another in its place.

AN APPLIED LESSON IN DISPLAY

The city loft of Mary Emmerling, measuring 1,800 square feet, brings to mind the wide open spaces of a country barn. In this unobstructed environment, objects rather than walls define areas for living, sleeping, and working.

Instead of one long flat space, levels were created by building up the living area and stepping down the kitchen space. A rag rug-covered sofa and homey collections are arranged in an intimate grouping, as if this particular area were naturally secluded from the rest. While the industrial details and

RAG RUG-COVERED SOFA *(left)* **represents a practical, long-wearing way of upholstering pieces in country style. The scrubbed pine table is not only functional but also an effective divider between the kitchen and living area.**

WOOD CHEESE RACK *(below),* **from a New Hampshire factory, is being reused as a storage shelf—this collector's alternative to conventional cabinets.**

PIGS.
FOR SALE

huge expanse of panel windows, cement floor, and glass block wall seemed uncompromising at first glance, the country pieces imposed the kind of warmth usually reserved for a cottage. The sleeping area, with traditional four-poster, is sequestered in an elevated corner near the bank of windows; the bath, where privacy was mandated, is secluded behind glass partitions and partial walls.

The compatibility between country and contemporary is exemplified in the kitchen. Here a pitch-black professional range is tempered by a patchwork rag rug whose red stripes match the glass knobs. A stainless-steel refrigerator is juxtaposed against a worn wood cabinet, and white walls are mellowed by apple and herb-drying baskets.

The successful display of country antiques and high-tech furnishings stems from the native simplicity and utilitarianism that both design idioms share.

The long wooden picnic-style table is a friendly place for parties and family dinners. The accompanying benches accommodate more guests than single chairs would. With the typical resourcefulness of a country collector, this city-dweller converted a damaged quilt into place mats.

COUNTRY ELEMENTS *(left)* warm a contemporary kitchen. An old wooden tub is filled with real vegetables and wood-carved replicas by contemporary folk artist Sherman Hensal.

BLUE-AND-WHITE SPONGEWARE *(right)*, all contemporary renditions, are illuminated by votive candles set in miniature ceramic plates.

ANTIQUE RAG RUGS and quilt-covered pillows establish Emmerling country in a city loft. An old church-shaped birdhouse serves as sculpture, as does a carved ram standing in front of the large window. The handmade twig chaise is covered in an old quilt.

Country pieces in an ultramodern bath are as soothing as a warm towel —they take the chill off. Rather than the standard accessories you'd expect to find in a 20th-century white-tiled bathroom, handcrafted objects were chosen as alternatives: an 18th-century wooden candle box to store tissue; an old peg rack to hold wooden mirrors (instead of sterile medicine cabinets); and baskets, mugs, and ceramic bowls to hold toiletries.

APPLE-DRYING RACK, antique wood containers, wreath, and child's chair are among unconventional elements that accent this modern bathroom.

MATCHING PINE MIRRORS *(above)* with heart-shaped motifs are suspended by rope from a long peg rack that also serves as a ledge for family mementos.

PEG RACK AND OLD SHELF *(far left)* are country fixtures that have been put to everyday use. The old shelf unit holds spiced potpourri; its aroma is intensified by steam from the bath.

BATHING IN AMERICAN COUNTRY *(left)* is enhanced by old bins, baskets, and grapevines.

Here are some closeup views of country details:

ANTIQUE SPICE CABINET *(above)* with squared drawers relates to white tiles.

BAY-LEAF WREATH *(right)* blends with cabinet in gray-green hue.

WOVEN SPLINT SEAT *(far right)* contrasts with textured floor covering.

PATCHWORK HOOKED RUG *(far left)*, mixing earth tones and bright colors, takes the stark edge off white cabinets in a sleekly modern design.

HOMESPUN BED LINENS *(left)* are in coordinating checked patterns and flag-waving colors of red, white, and blue.

161

ANTIQUE PEG RACK serves as an open-air storage unit for drying herbs and hanging candles with meat hooks. This kind of rack can also be used in the bathroom to hold towels, or in the bedroom as a catchall for scarves, belts, or necklaces.

The harmonious mix of old and new defies any standard formula for displaying collections. This particular scheme draws on a highly personal formula for its success: spaces are clearly defined with collections of related objects housed in white recessed shelves; important country pieces are positioned as room dividers and create a sense of order in a space that has no walls to define it.

SHELVES OF SLIPWARE (far left), a discreet built-in unit, act as a room divider flanked by an old cupboard.

GRASS WREATH (left) hangs near a matched set of pantry boxes, a tin kerosene lamp with original paint, and tin animals by contemporary artist Ivan Barnett.

COMB-PAINTED FLOOR (above) represents an old technique traditionally applied to wood surfaces. In this case, it has been applied to a cement floor. Its pattern was modeled after the wavy lines of Lester Breininger's slipware. Glass brick walls—signs of the loft's industrial past—filter light and assure privacy.

165

PENCIL-POST BED is an 18th-century style of four-poster, which provides a private chamber without conventional bedroom walls. It's dressed with a homespun canopy and linen curtains to filter light from the nearby window. Spice chest on the bedside table houses jewelry in its separate compartments.

CHAPTER 5

Living with Collections

*A collector's terrain spans the highways and byways of America's countryside. There are no boundaries to deter the collector in quest of a new find, no flea market too remote to track down. But **the ultimate destination is home,** where **collections express the passions and fancies of their owner** and where visual pleasures extend the emotional rewards. Here is **a look inside some of those welcoming homes.***

To accommodate an expanding collection of American Indian art, Peggy and Forest Fenn transformed a primitive adobe into a home gallery built of wood beams and timbers from nine old barns in Northern New Mexico. In fact, dimensions of the new rooms were determined by the lengths of salvaged roof beams. Each ceiling is made of different native woods, including salt cedar, aspen, split cedar, spruce, and willow. Even the cabinets are constructed of seasoned wood—a half century old.

Rooms with softly contoured walls and archways are illuminated primarily by skylights creating an atmosphere somewhat like the subterranean Kivas of the Pueblo Indians. And the artifacts contained within are the legacies of pre-reservation tribes who left an indelible mark on American history, and whose intricate handwork enriches the lives of these modern-day collectors.

Forest Fenn is an ex-fighter pilot whose infatuation with art began just over a decade ago. That his home/gallery complex has quadrupled in size since 1972 attests to a thriving business in American and Indian art.

Fenn's affinity for Indian artifacts stems from his Boy Scout days in Texas where he began collecting arrowheads. Raised in a frugal atmosphere, he took to making his own toys with the spirit of a pioneer and the resourcefulness of an entrepreneur. "I remember one whole summer making marbles," says Fenn, "grinding them down by hand. I'd get agate up in Montana and Wyoming along the rivers. Everyone wanted all my agates."

Amassing objects that others covet has evolved into a profit-making situation, for the Fenn Gallery attracts

OLD WAGON WHEELS *(preceding pages)* mark the entrance to the Santa Fe, New Mexico, adobe of Peggy and Forest Fenn. Here and in an adjoining guesthouse, a vast assortment of Indian artifacts are integrated with Southwestern design elements that span three centuries.

TOMAHAWKS, SADDLEBAGS, TACKED BELTS *(left),* as well as knife sheaths, Plains Indian moccasins, and hundreds of artifacts and items of clothing, are suspended from old beams in Forest Fenn's home office: early bow-and-arrow sets and spears fill one corner.

171

a worldwide clientele. And its owner seems to have achieved the best of both worlds—home is a benevolent environment for his store of culture.

"I came out here to build a little Indian store, so I could collect Indian things," recalls Fenn, whose goal has clearly been fulfilled, if not exceeded.

ZUÑI, TESUQUE, AND HOPI POTTERY *(far left)* date from the mid-1800s. A hanging piece of horizontal reeds is a tepee chair or backrest from the Northern Plains, c. 1880. In the *nicho* below is an 1840 Zuñi water olla. The hanging piece with beaded floral and geometric design is a Sioux saddlebag.

FUR TRADE ARTIFACTS *(above left)* span the years from 1725 to 1850 and cover the breadth of ornamentation exchanged. In the upper right: quilled red armbands with feathers. Right of center: a round ornament with eagle feathers and tanned Crow Indian scalp. Left of center: long bone hair-pipe necklaces and early French brass trade beads. Far left: a hair ornament of horsetail with quilled bangles. Among the other articles are silver gorgets and Indian peace medals.

ANTIQUE KACHINAS AND HISTORIC POTS *(center left)* line a library that also houses a quilled eagle-feather dance bustle, eleven eagle bonnets from 1860 to 1890, and shelves of first-edition histories and archaeological volumes.

KIOWA AND COMANCHE BEADED BAGS *(bottom left)* surround early Apache awl cases with tin jangles.

Forest Fenn shares his living quarters with some 1,400 objects from another civilization. A connoisseur of Indian artifacts, he is also an art dealer whose thriving business evolved from a modest collection begun just eight years ago. Fenn's sprawling adobe functions as a public and private gallery where Indian relics have expanded to fill the vast space allotted to them. Not everything is for sale, however. Fenn tends to keep "the best pieces" for himself. He is constantly adding outstanding work as

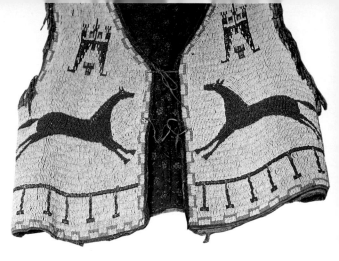

QUILLED AND BEADED DOCTOR BAGS *(left),* **from the Northern Plains Indians, 1870 to 1890.**

BEADED VEST *(right),* **c. 1880, is a Plains Indian artifact with horse motif front and back.**

MAYAN AND PUEBLO PAINTED JUGS *(below)* **are joined by a polychrome jug, third from left, by Maria and Julian Martinez.**

EAGLE-FEATHER BONNETS from the Northern Plains Indians and early Hopi and Zuñi kachinas are displayed under the old beams of the Fenns' guesthouse library.

he finds it, opening up new space for each acquisition. He tends to place related projects together, so that items are cataloged when displayed; for instance, moccasins, pipe bags, painted buffalo robes, and feather bonnets are displayed together.

Even though some objects hang on overhead beams, every piece is within easy reach for closer inspection. "Nothing is untouchable," he says. "I will hang objects if it is possible, so as to conserve space. I like to hang them from beams on cup hooks using shower curtain holders so that each can be removed with a hook stick."

Fenn favors white as the most effective background color, claiming it emphasizes details and textures of his artifacts. As for illumination, he prefers subdued, low-voltage lighting

for a soft glow at a safe distance from perishable collections. All objects are protected from the harsh glare of the desert sun.

**PIPES AND PIPE BAGS *(above)*
hang on a white-walled space, attached by hooks to ceiling beams. Some are beaded, some quilled; one has human scalps.**

PORTUGUESE WOODEN GATE *(far left)*, 17th century, serves as a headboard for this bed covered in Bayeta blankets.

ORNAMENTAL SHIELDS *(left)*, from the early Plains Indians and Southwestern Pueblo tribes, span the years from 1750 to 1900.

179

MIXING COUNTRY FLAVORS

This particular kitchen, in a house in Ohio shown on the following pages, demonstrates how a comprehensive but carefully edited collection of country pieces is integrated into a dining area whose decoration is derived from an orderly display of old implements.

For the collector whose love of harmony and order is evident in this kitchen (and in the Shaker room on page 186), decorating is a by-product of comfort. That comfortable feeling results from a "layering" of styles that seem to have a kinship with one another. So we find Shaker pieces sitting side by side with New England Windsor chairs in a room that is neither museumlike in purity nor overly cluttered with a random assortment of objects. Its comfort, in fact, is visual as well as physical.

BASKETS *(above)*, from miniature to bucket-sized, hang from old meat hooks attached to ceiling beams.

MID-1800s UTENSIL RACK *(right)* hangs over a Shaker bread-rising cupboard on which old pantry boxes and contemporary wood carvings are displayed.

SHAKER CUPBOARD *(left)*, an early 19th-century woodbox with original blue paint, mixes with early 1800s Windsor chairs and painted table. The chandelier is a contemporary piece, made from old wood, by Lieutenant Moses Willard of Madeira, Ohio. Fireplace tools are wrought-iron Shaker pieces and late 1800s brass ladles from Canton, Ohio.

While the Shakers didn't intend to teach future generations how to decorate, they did leave a legacy of superb craftsmanship and respect for the humblest objects. The settings here are directly descended from Shaker rooms where pegboards held items of daily use, cupboards and boxes contained perishables, and tables were simplified to the essential four legs and a flat surface of modest proportions.

WALNUT SLANT-FRONT DESK *(below)* and Shaker weaver's chair are the major elements in a work corner. The overhead pegboard, which acts as a decorative molding, supports Shaker baskets, a clothes hanger, and an antique print.

TALL CHEST *(right)* is a butternut piece from the Enfield, New Hampshire, Shaker community, and the owners' first purchase. While the child's chair and table to the right are not Shaker, their simple lines adhere to those of the basic country pieces in this group.

PAINTED TABLE *(far right)* holds a rare basket, signed by the sister who made it. Pegboard display of small Shaker pieces includes candle holder, barometer, miniature chair, and embroidery hoop with hanks of yarn.

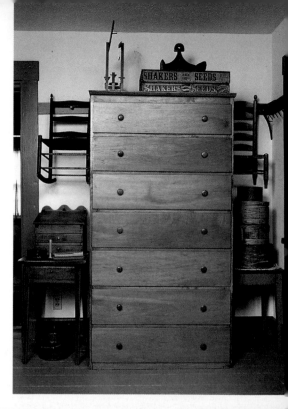

Finely crafted furniture such as the Shakers produced is even more outstanding in a white-walled room with delicately stenciled borders.

TIGER MAPLE BED *(right),* c. 1820 from Ohio, is a country cabinetmaker's interpretation of Sheraton and Empire styles. An 18th-century rake-back cupboard with original blue paint adds one note of color to the room, picked up by a candlewick-stitched coverlet draped over the bedpost. Complementing the simple furnishings is an early 19th-century comb-back Windsor chair.

SHAKER ARTIFACTS *(below)* include vegetable-dyed boxes with characteristic "lappers," the finger-shaped joiners. An 1886 almanac is among the assortment of miniatures and memorabilia.

SHAKER SEED CHEST *(below right)* bears a label attributing it to the Mount Lebanon settlement. This rare piece has a marbleized paper veneer and porcelain pulls.

Shaker, for many collectors, is a state of mind. The finely tuned furniture and accessories evoke images of the simple life and of orderly rooms where each possession was revered for its craftsmanship.

TIN AND STONEWARE CONTAINERS *(below left)* were used to store butter and to ripen cheese. They stand on a mid-1800s Shaker herb chest.

SHAKER SEED BOXES *(below center)* sit atop a chest.

SHAKER CHAIR *(below)* is the slat-back rocker originally made in the Mount Lebanon, New York, community after 1875. Sold by mail, this #4 design was priced at $7. It features the webbed seat (called "listing") characteristic of Shaker chairs. The red fabric picks up the dominant color in the Shaker rag rug.

Decorating in the Shaker style is a matter of paring down to the essentials of living—a few well-chosen pieces provide necessary comfort. The room illustrated here reflects that simplicity and eloquence. The resident, a connoisseur of Shaker design, began her collection with one tall chest from the Enfield, New Hampshire, community. It has grown to include fine examples of Shaker chairs, a desk, an 1830s signed sampler, and a footstool from the Shaker community in Mount Lebanon, New York.

SHAKER ANTIQUES *(left)* appear in an appropriately simple setting of white walls, painted molding, and painted wood floors.

WALNUT SHAKER SECRETARY *(below)* with porcelain knobs is an early 1800s piece. A candle box, apple peeler, and bottle filler are among the handcrafted Shaker implements that adorn it.

AN OCTAGONAL GALLERY FOR FOLK ART

Bernard Barenholtz bought his first piece of folk art—a toy milk wagon—as a birthday gift for his wife. That discovery was followed by hundreds more, which have yielded enormous tangible as well as emotional rewards. When his collection reached museumlike proportions, Mr. Barenholtz decided to build separate

WEATHER VANE AND OUTDOOR ORNAMENTS *(left)* announce this collector's affection for folk art. Situated in an entrance hall, the large metal objects can still be viewed in the context of outdoors but are protected from the elements by this glass enclosure. The weather vane, a rendering of a man on horseback, and the Liberty figure—both made of copper with gold leaf—were manufactured by the Cushing Company in the late 1870s. The

copper finial is thought to have decorated a public building in turn-of-the-century Kansas City, Missouri. Such architectural ornaments, salvaged from old buildings, are increasingly sought after as indoor decorations and are emerging as a new form of folk art.

TIN TOYS *(below)* from the 1870s and 1880s parade on narrow white shelves suited to their miniature dimensions.

189

FOLK ART HAVEN provides ample display space for collections on walls, floors, shelves, and balcony. The stylish seating arrangement includes Mies van der Rohe's Barcelona chairs.

192

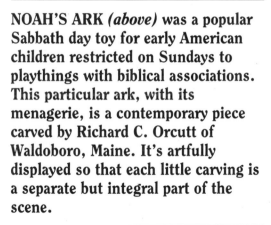

NOAH'S ARK (above) was a popular Sabbath day toy for early American children restricted on Sundays to playthings with biblical associations. This particular ark, with its menagerie, is a contemporary piece carved by Richard C. Orcutt of Waldoboro, Maine. It's artfully displayed so that each little carving is a separate but integral part of the scene.

WEATHER VANES (left) seem to float on high walls of the light-filled gallery.

---

quarters where the toys and primitive art would have no competition from the furnishings and normal clutter of a household. This was not to be an isolated chamber but an extension of his farmhouse.

The two-story octagonal building that evolved is, in his words, "a living area to house a collection." Appended to his farmhouse, the structure contains a bedroom and bath. But the pristine collection of antique weather vanes, whirligigs, signs, and tin, wood, and cast-iron toys is the undisputed focal point: the decor, accordingly, is minimal—white walls, narrow white shelves, unobtrusive pedestals, and bare wood floors.

"Folk art pieces, particularly the small sculptural and mechanical ones, are really toys," according to Barenholtz, whose home is a grown-ups' wonderland. "Grown-ups design and make toys for themselves," he says. "Whimseys, for example, were made by adults for their own amusement, but were often passed off as amusements for children."

The restful, uncrowded atmosphere that pervades the Barenholtz home indicates a quiet regard—if not reverence—for the hundreds of objects contained indoors and also in the surrounding broad meadow.

193

1824.

WHIRLIGIGS mounted on white
stages take on the attitude of puppets
in motion, some with flailing arms.
Carvings date from 1880s; the
armless man, 1850–1860.

TAVERN SIGN *(above)* is documented in 19th-century records. N. Brown was granted a license to operate a tavern in Haverhill, Massachusetts, about 1823.

FLAG-WAVING WHIRLIGIG *(above center)* is a three-way action toy, beginning with the hand crank; when the propeller is set in motion, the flag waves.

ROCKING HORSES *(right)* take on the stature of important artwork, set against white walls and open space. The bentwood design at left, c. 1860, could pass for a contemporary sculpture. More common among folk art rocking horses were those first styles made from packing crates in the early to mid-1800s. The one at right, bred from a United States Bazaar Company crate, has an oilcloth seat with burlap padding.

CIGAR-SMOKING SAM *(facing page, above right)* stood on the counter of a tobacco shop in Pottsville, Pennsylvania, about 1875.

PUNCH FIGURE *(above left)* is a trade sign from the 19th century, supposedly for a tobacco wholesaler in Danbury, Connecticut. Punch figures, like American Indians, were used in front of tobacco shops and wholesalers. They were often holding a stack of cigars or a tobacco leaf.

DIORAMA *(above center)* is a contemporary piece by Orcutt, a carver from Maine. It was inspired by Edward Hicks.

WOODEN EAGLE *(above right)* is attributed to John Haley Bellamy, famed 19th-century carver from Kittery, Maine.

"After two, you have a collection," says Bernard Barenholtz, whose inventory of antique toys has swelled to fill 3,500 square feet of space in the octagonal building adjoining his 1875 New England farmhouse. The two-story gallery houses a collection of primitive toys and folk art figures that spans nearly a quarter of a century, displayed in an all-white, bare wood floor environment illuminated by narrow windows carved into the building's eight sides. The slit windows were designed to allow in "slivers of light way up high," and to keep out great quantities of sunlight, which would fade or dry the numerous painted pieces.

While the number of objects has grown enough to fill several museums, Mr. Barenholtz displays only about one-third at a time, so that each whirligig, mechanical toy, or carved animal is not overshadowed by others of its kind. Objects stand on their own, elevated on white pedestals, surrounded by ample amounts of white space, or are sensitively arranged on shelves or other surfaces. Mr. Barenholtz's carefully edited displays reveal the hand of a passionate collector whose museum-quality pieces are treated with intelligence and respect. For Bernard Barenholtz, living with folk art is a way of life.

TOYS ON SHELVES *(above)* **include Pennsylvania carving of a man with cigar on horseback** *(center shelf, second from right)*. **Carved wood horses** *(top shelf)*, **from the 1880s, were found in Maine and Connecticut.**

PAIR OF PORTRAITS *(left)*, **circa 1845, are unsigned works by Joseph Whiting Stock. The paintings are documented in the artist's diary and their subjects identified as Mary and Francis Wilcox of Springfield, Massachusetts. The toys below are the same as those in the portraits. (The doll's dress had been changed.)**

BUILT FOR COLLECTIONS

When one old basket increases to a dozen, and a few early wood carvings grow into a crowd, how do you accommodate them all? One irrepressible collector actually built a capacious house with antiques in mind. The New England saltbox, a style in keeping with the antiques' colonial roots, derives its decoration from orderly arrangements of related objects. Each room features groups of country pieces unified into interesting vignettes: baskets hang from kitchen beams, pottery lines country cupboards, wood carvings fill a spare corner. Were these same items to be

dispersed throughout the house, clutter would likely result. Instead, there is order and thoughtful integration of antiques in rooms appropriate for their use.

A sense of order is also achieved from background color, particularly if many wood tones appear in one room. White walls, for example, emphasize individual items rather than compete with them. In a rustic setting such as this, white serves to define the space and provides a welcome lightness.

KITCHEN COLLECTIONS *(far left)* **fill a painted cupboard; old baskets hang by meat hooks from beams.**

IRON SNOWBIRDS *(left)* **trim the roof of the saltbox and prevent snow from dropping.**

OLD COBBLER'S BENCH *(below),* **late 1800s, has storage space for tools. Bootmakers' trade signs are displayed on the wall.**

Collectors usually gravitate toward objects of related origins and similar use. A basket fancier, for example, will search high and low for one special basket to add a new dimension to an existing collection. That culling process can take years, for collections evolve, they don't just happen. What may come as a surprise are the number of like pieces you have spread about the house. Perhaps you have one pair of old candle holders on the mantel, another on the dining table, and still another on a foyer chest. Taking inventory would reveal a

collection by most standards. Grouping all the candle holders in one spot, as this collector did, is an emphatic way of decorating with collections, as this setting illustrates.

HOG-SCRAPER CANDLESTICKS, c. 1800, so named for their resemblance to scrapers that removed bristles from hogs, are grouped as if to celebrate coming together in the 20th century. Originally they were hooked to the backs of chairs for over-the-shoulder illumination.

A few well-chosen pieces in unexpected places can have a miraculous effect on a room. By positioning folk art on crossbeams, old jugs on top of cabinets, whirligigs and weather vanes in forgotten niches and corners, this collector expanded serviceable space.

DECORATED STONEWARE *(above)* sits atop the cabinets in a country laundry room. A step-up shelf arrangement was built for display.

WEATHER VANES, ROCKING HORSES *(far left),* and folk art pieces transform a soaring space into an intimate gallery, which is also used as a dining area.

OLD LAUNDRY ITEMS *(left),* including wash sticks and a wringer lamp, add charm to an ordinary utility room.

205

FOUR-POSTER BED with Williamsburg checked canopy was copied from a late 18th-century design. Nearby are contemporary folk art carvings, country pieces, and early 19th-century hand-blown glass bottles.

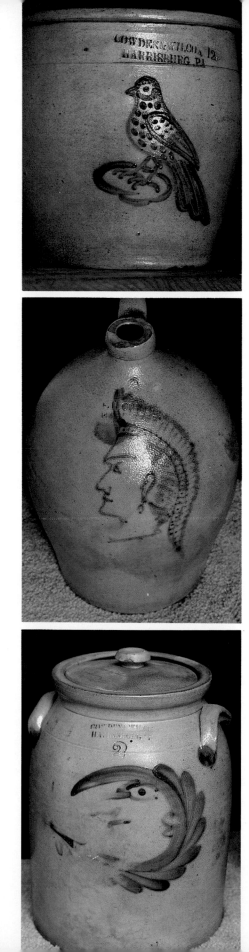

Cupboards, the mainstay of old colonial homes, are utilitarian fixtures with a decorative disposition. Cupboards with doors can function as closets, protecting fragile stoneware and glass from breakage and dust, and can provide a hiding place or a public display, depending on how the doors are positioned. Open cupboards offer shelf space for innumerable types of collections, with built-in compartments that can serve as well for quilts as for pottery. Corner cupboards monopolize those angles that might otherwise be considered wasted space. Furthermore, they contribute to a room's character, just as recessed windows and rustic beams do. Because of their angled position, corner cupboards and their contents are visible from all vantage points—and thus are an integral part of a room's decoration. This collector has clearly made the most of cupboard space.

STONEWARE AND REDWARE *(far left)* **fill a mid-1800s corner cupboard and an early 19th-century Norwegian chest whose bottom shelves house antique quilts.**

STORAGE CONTAINER *(top left),* **of salt-glazed stoneware, was stamped by its 19th-century maker, Cowden & Wilcox of Harrisburg, Pennsylvania. It once held molasses or honey.**

STONEWARE JUG *(center left),* **marked F. H. Cowden, Harrisburg, Pennsylvania, was probably used for storing vinegar.**

COVERED CROCK *(below left),* **also from the Cowden & Wilcox Company, was likely a container for butter.**

GALENA POTTERY *(below)* **was made in Galena, Illinois, during the mid-1800s. Instead of displaying the collection against a contrasting background, the owner placed the earth-toned pottery on a similarly colored chest. While a dark background is not the conventional way to set off dark objects, this example proves that a break from conventional wisdom can make for decorating success.**

IRON WINDMILL WEIGHTS from the late 1800s were originally used to regulate the speed of windmill turns. The weights now decorate the railings of this New England saltbox deck.

A HOME FOR REGIONAL ART

Certain folk art speaks of specific regions, such as Navajo rugs from the Southwest or colonial wares from the Northeast. Hannelis and Horst Kuntze's North Carolina home celebrates folk art of the area, including baskets, decoys, and pottery. The collections appear in groups throughout the house, arranged according to material—wood, iron, and clay.

Their pottery includes an important collection of face jugs, contemporary versions of the traditional Southern art form. Given prominent position in a glass-walled room that meshes with the outdoors, the face jugs are the work of Southern artists Lanier Meaders and Burlon Craig. Also called grotesque jugs, these pottery forms appeal for their realism—an antidote to what these collectors call "cuteness" in some folk art. "Nobody is perfect, and it shows in these face jugs. The smile may be crooked," says Hannelis, "and that's the way people really look."

The face jugs make an emphatic sculptural statement when massed in groups around the house. Other pieces—quilts, baskets, early crocks—have been arranged in equally inventive fashion, on floors, windowsills, and mantels; over and under furniture; in open cupboards and closets. "For me, a piece has to be in the right place," she says. "If it doesn't have a right place, I don't put it out."

TWIG BIRDHOUSES *(left)*, miniature chairs, Navajo rug,

sculptural hearth, and a collection of regional pottery fill this airy living room. The face jugs, also known as grotesque jugs, are thought to have originated in Africa, possibly as a type of voodoo.

SEMINOLE INDIAN DOLLS *(below)*, from Florida, are grouped in a North Carolina twig basket. The dolls wear authentic beads and dresses.

213

Integrating collections into a room's design can mean stationing pieces in obvious places such as cupboards and shelf units. Another approach—positioning objects in unlikely places—contains the element of surprise.

These collectors, for instance, chose an unpredictable spot for displaying their Southern pottery: on and under an antique wooden bench and on top of an ornate chest whose formality is playfully mocked by the crowd of face jugs.

RYE STRAW BASKETS *(above)* **from Pennsylvania and North Carolina, 1850 to 1910, were used by early settlers for rising dough.**

FACE JUGS *(left)* **peer out from underneath an antique bench and take up one seat. The bottom group is swirl pottery with alkaline glaze, by North Carolina potter B. B. Craig. The seated group is black-glazed, by Georgia potter Lanier Meaders.**

HAND-PAINTED CUPBOARD *(right),* **c. 1760, is from Austria. The primitive-looking face jugs on top are in contrast to its ornate detail.**

One way to display a collection is to line the pieces up according to graduated sizes. The objects look tidy and, as illustrated in this North Carolina home, have a cumulative effect.

ANTIQUE FURNITURE AND FOLK ART *(above)* in this dining room include early North Carolina kitchen table, redware, and pewter. Alkaline-glazed Southern pottery stands on the windowsill. Old North Carolina trivets, ladles, and forks are among the kitchen tools that decorate one wall. The hand-carved wooden oxen on the table were made by a contemporary craftsman.

DUCK DECOYS AND OLD JUGS *(right)* are arranged in graduated sizes on shelves. The wood carvings date from the late 1800s; some of them are signed by their makers or are still wearing their original coats of paint. Old jugs, decorated with dark green alkaline glaze and dating from the 1800s to 1920s, were once storage containers for liquids.

216

A PROPER PLACE FOR COLLECTIONS

In a town called Canal Winchester, Ohio, is an 1837 brick house that could be filled to the rafters, Rube Goldberg fashion, with collections stuffing every room. Instead the owners, Betty and Jim Murray, have composed their varied antiques and contemporary crafts into harmonious arrangements of small- and large-scaled objects, surrounded by generous amounts of space. Symmetry is an obvious consideration here: five hog-scraper candle holders line each side of the mantel; the tall cupboard is balanced by a wood-framed sampler, towel rack, and stacks of Shaker boxes on the opposite side; centered between two matching sofas (made by a local craftsman) are a contemporary folk painting, bench, and hooked hemp rug. Even the crowd of Teddy bears is well organized, with big bears supporting little ones in what appears to be a display of great affection.

TEDDY BEARS *(left),* 160 strong, are thoughtfully arranged in a close-knit family, with the smallest supported by larger members of the species.

AMERICAN CRAFTS *(below)* include old hog-scraper candlesticks, Shaker boxes, and cupboard, c. 1860. The shelves hold a collection of 18th-century homespun bedticks and New England blankets. The old wooden bench is newly decorated with a "Peaceable Kingdom" scene by Ohio artist Judith Key.

LANDMARK HOUSE, c. 1837 *(below),* **was built by Sarah and John Summerhill and completely restored by the present owners, whose collections are in keeping with the colonial architecture.**

BAIL-HANDLE PANTRY BOXES
show the range of old paint, gray and
robin's-egg blue being the rarest
colors for boxes of this type. Less
common than the handleless pantry
boxes, these were made in the
Northeast from about 1700 to 1880.
The owner lines them with plastic
containers in which she stores spices,
sugar, and flour.

Blankets and pantry boxes, two types of collections that introduce a range of color, pattern, and texture, can be particularly decorative when stacked in an attractive arrangement.

STACKS OF HOMESPUN *(below)* **make a vivid display in a plain cupboard. In addition to being decorative, the linen and cotton bedticks are used frequently as spreads and tablecloths.**

STEP-BACK CUPBOARD IN MUSTARD PAINT *(right)* **from New England, c. 1820, is filled with bail-handle pantry buckets. Pantry boxes form a colorful pillar in the corner; the carefully composed assortment is the fruit of a six-year search. Dated as early as 1664, the boxes all have their original paint. The stack of rectangular boxes includes a mustard-yellow blanket box from New England. On top is a bear handmade from an old coverlet. A large Shaker field basket, used to carry lunches to workers, stands atop the cupboard. Hanging from the pegboard is a niddy noddy, the wooden device once used to wind yarn to measure a skein.**

AMISH APRONS, 1840–1880, found in Ohio and Pennsylvania, drape a wall with homespun fabric in typically muted colors. The aprons, shaped by hand-carved wooden hangers, each seem to project a distinct personality. Baskets above give the illusion of height to the room.

The playful nature of some collections leads quite naturally to playful arrangements. In this house, the bear kingdom is a playroom for nine grandchildren. Known as the Bear Room to the Murray clan, it welcomes small visitors to share in the activity of its full-time inhabitants. Clothed by the owner, bears are recruited to push wagons, handle an ironing board, tackle a miniature sewing machine, and even ride "bearback."

ANTIQUE DOLLS *(right)* congregate in carriages in a hallway where they can be viewed by passersby.

ROOM OF BEARS *(far right)* is a collector's playland for visiting grandchildren.

OLD BEARS *(below)* include a Steiff, c. 1893, with replacement button eyes and sailor suit.

The resourcefulness displayed by early settlers is a trait that modern collectors seem to have inherited. Splint baskets, originally constructed to carry produce from the fields, are now being used to display collectors' bounty at home. Woven frames that once supported mattresses on early beds have been elevated to another level of usefulness—as ceiling racks for drying herbs. Peg racks that sufficed as closets for the Shakers are decorative tools for 20th-century collectors. It may be that we've come full circle at this point in history, by taking the best of the past and reusing it in brand-new ways.

BASKETS FILLED WITH CLOTH CATS *(left),* **1844–1900, stand upright so that they can function as frames, the contents of which change according to the collector's whim. The chunky wood mantel also provides a ledge for drying herbs, as does the overhead rafter.**

HERB GARDEN *(below)* **furnishes a bountiful supply of fresh herbs. The garden is laid out with bricks taken from a nearby site where an old house once stood. The herbs include parsley, chives, sage, creeping thyme, tansy, comfrey, and a Bible plant.**

A MARY CHRISTMAS

To me, there is nothing more wonderful than an old-fashioned Christmas, and my loft is proof that you don't have to be in the country to enjoy it. Come Christmas, my city home is transformed into a celebration of traditional decorations and favorite possessions, with a few special touches.

Samantha, nine, and Jonathan, six, are in charge of decorating the tree. The ornaments we use were made by folk artist Nancy Thomas, whose ornaments have decorated the White House tree. My green-painted North Carolina cupboard gets special treatment, too. I put the Nancy Thomas angels on top and, on the stepback, two Santa Clauses by Larry Koosed (another contemporary folk artist), along with my hog-scraper candlesticks and pine boughs.

I can't say enough in favor of candles. I use them all year long, but at Christmas I go all out. I put little white votive candles everywhere—in tin molds shaped like stars, in wooden candle holders, in fresh cored apples, in my collection of bowls. The effect is wonderful. Christmas is the festival of lights, and there's no better time to get out your candles and put them around the house.

CARVED SANTAS are by contemporary folk artist Larry Koosed; tin deer, by Ivan Barnett; mulberry wreath with carved wood birds, by Nancy Thomas; iron bird and star are decoys from an old shooting gallery. They are displayed on a late 1800s cupboard, a rare example in its original pale shade of paint.

231

I love to dress up the entrance to my loft, so when people come to visit they'll sense a warm, personal welcome. I enjoy mixing old pieces with my folk art—and modern elements, like the glass block wall that forms my entryway. The floor just happens to be Christmas green, a color that gives me pleasure throughout the year. It was comb-painted by Richard Lowell Neas in a folk art type of plaid. The floor is actually industrial cement which appears carpeted with the textured design that the artist applied.

TAVERN TABLE *(right)*, early 18th century, decorates the entrance hall. It's laden with wooden pull toys and contemporary versions of pierced lampshades on pottery bases. Tiny lights are wrapped around a ficus tree set into a basket. A folk art watermelon sits below the table.

CONTEMPORARY REDWARE *(below)* by Lester Breininger is in holiday dress with pine branches, holly, and pottery cups filled with votive candles.

The reds and greens of carved wood watermelons and the bright patches of primary color on quilts seem made for Christmas and folk art joins the merriment. Since not everybody has a mantel on which to put traditional trimmings, I suggest using a peg rack to hang stockings and little gifts. And as an alternative to traditional Christmas wrappings, place gifts in old baskets and tins, then tie with ribbons. For the most personal touch of all, fill the baskets and tins with homemade treats, fresh fruit, or nuts.

OLD SHAKER BASKET *(above)*, used for drying cheese or herbs, stands behind wood-carved and hand-painted angels by Nancy Thomas.

CHRISTMAS VIGNETTE *(right)*: child's homespun dress with miniature wreath of mulberry vines and berries. Stocking is an old quilt piece with a crocheted cuff, trimmed with heart pillow sachets made from old blankets.

FOLK ART PULL TOY *(center right)* grazes in a Christmas pine setting.

PAPER SANTA ORNAMENTS *(far right)* are contemporary copies of old greeting cards—and a very important collectible now.

234

Green-painted furniture, red-and-white quilts, lots of candles, and folk art toys are things I live with all year. When Christmas comes, I arrange pine boughs, string berries with my children, and lace everything with the berry string. I don't have to add much more than the evergreens, pinecones, cranberry ropes, more candles, and the space turns festive. In fact, the loft hardly looks like the same place it was before.

Samantha and Jonathan use all their special toys and crafts they've made at school to decorate under the tree. I hang up stockings sewn from old bits of quilt and make sure that every piece of furniture and folk art has been bedecked in finery and assumes a holiday look.

MERRY CHRISTMAS PLATE *(left)* is slipware by Lester Breininger. The heart quilt on the wall is from Pennsylvania. The carved Santa, ram, and treetop angel *(below)* is by Nancy Thomas.

Friends who stop by at Christmastime get a present to take home—cinnamon sticks tied up with a homespun heart; a little basket filled with fruit and nuts, trimmed with red ribbon. *Anything* in a basket makes a wonderful present; just add holly and a bow. Sometimes, instead of a real apple, I'll put in a wooden one—a piece of folk art to remind you of Christmas all year long.

Fun ornaments like those carved wood Santa Clauses and angels are being made again. The look is "old," but the pieces are contemporary. I think we will see a lot more handcrafted work—these are the "antiques of the future." For me, it is part of that wonderful, from the heart caring that Christmas—and American Country—are all about.

CARVED WOOD WATERMELONS *(above)* **by Felipe Archuleta say country and the colors say Christmas** —add pine branches and the glow of a candle to say "Merry Country Christmas."

OLD BASKETS *(above right)* **are filled with healthful goodies, nuts, lady apples, and oranges, then tied up with red ribbons and cinnamon sticks to make wonderful presents. The heart candle holder is by Jerome Livingwood; homespun heart by local artist Barbara Kelley.**

RED AND WHITE QUILT TEDDY BEARS *(right)* mingle with gifts and folk art. To dress up pinecones, mix them in a bowl with cranberry ropes, entwined with tiny white lights.

STOCKINGS *(far right),* hung from the window with care, are hand-sewn from old quilt tops. Hearts are pieced together from scraps of old blankets.

PAPIER-MÂCHÉ SANTAS, from the early 1900s, were collected at antiques shows across the country. They are gathered on top of a country chest.

Directory

OF CONTEMPORARY SOURCES

The "Directory of Contemporary Sources" lists stores specializing in country furniture, folk art, artifacts, and accessories. Many of these reproductions and adaptations are less expensive than their antique counterparts and are generally more readily available. These items are frequently handcrafted and possess a distinctly individual quality that reflects the current interest in arts and crafts. Some of the stores that appear in this directory sell antiques as well as contemporary pieces. It is always advisable to call or write for shopping information.

ALASKA

Country Classics
934 West Sixth
Anchorage, Alaska 99501
(907)276-2148
New quilts, handmade American baskets, wool and 100 percent rag rugs, cotton fabrics, country accent pieces, including weather vanes, pottery, tinware; a selection of books on quilting, stenciling, and folk art.

CALIFORNIA

Ames Gallery
2661 Cedar Street (at La Loma)
Berkeley, Calif. 94708
(415)845-4949
American folk art and artifacts, contemporary folk painting and sculpture, and the work of contemporary California artists.

Raggedy Baby
3356 Sacramento
San Francisco, Calif. 94803
Antique furniture and accessories.

Stockfleth-Disston
381 Hayes Street
San Francisco, Calif. 94102
(415)864-1244
Designers and manufacturers of furniture, including sideboards, harvest tables, room-dividing screens; a selection of baskets.

CONNECTICUT

Connecticut River Artisans
Cooperative
Goodspeed Landing
East Haddam, Conn. 06423
Mailing Address: P.O. Box 155
East Haddam, Conn. 06423
(203)873-1661
Weaving, baskets, pewter, dollhouses, bisque dolls, folk art toys, quilts, wooden weather vanes, floorcloths, and fireboards.

Country Folk
277 Tokeneke Road
Darien, Conn. 06820
(203)655-6887
Antiques, folk art, quilts, country accessories, and reproduction furniture.

Ian Ingersoll
Main Street
West Cornwall, Conn. 06796
(203)672-6334
Cabinet and chair maker.

Main Street Merchants
12 Main Street North
Woodbury, Conn. 06798
(203)263-0771
Contemporary folk art, country home furnishings, wallpapers, and accessories.

Anita Miller
Hemslojd Ltd.
P.O. Box 643
182 Ridgefield Road
Wilton, Conn. 06897
(203)762-9560 or (203)762-9235
Country rugs, handwoven, with borders of hearts, flowers, or allover block designs.

DELAWARE

American in Old New Castle
408 Delaware Street
New Castle, Del. 19720
(302)322-6408
Country reproductions, folk art, and country antiques.

IDAHO

The Quilt Barn
421 South River and Elm
Box 1252
Hailey, Idaho 83333
(208)788-4011
Quilts made
to order.

Rustic Revival
672 North Dearborn
Chicago, Ill. 60610
(312)337-5932
Contemporary American painted
wooden folk art and handcrafts; gypsy
willow twig furniture and
reproduction country pine furniture.

ILLINOIS

Country Cousin
8 West 1st Street
Hinsdale, Ill. 60521
(312)655-1567
Country accessories and folk art,
including tin lighting, rag rugs,
baskets, stoneware, herbs, quilts, and
coverlets.

Flower Mill Inc.
302 South 3rd Street
Geneva, Ill. 60134
(312)232-8803
Country pine and oak furniture and
collectibles.

Barbara and Fred Johnson
Clock Tower Inn
7801 East State Street
Box 5285
I-90 Tollway and Bus. 20
Rockford, Ill. 61125
(815)397-6699
Antique furniture, accessories, and
contemporary folk art; carvings by Lou
Shifferl.

The Ollde Mill
231 East Lincoln Highway
De Kalb, Ill. 60115
(815)758-6614
Handcrafted country reproductions
and accessories from the Appalachian
Mountain area of Georgia and
Tennessee.

INDIANA

Rebecca Haarer
Haarer's Quaint Shop
Uptown Business District
Shipshewana, Ind. 46565
Mailing Address:
Box 52
Shipshewana, Ind. 46565
(219)768-4787
Objects distinctive of the area
produced by a group of cottage
industries in contemporary styles or as
historical reproduction.

KANSAS

Antiques American
5107 Linden
Roeland Park, Kan. 66203
(a suburb of Kansas City, Mo.)
(913)262-5114
Country pine furniture, primitive
accessories, and folk art reproductions.

KENTUCKY

By Bee Pottery
P.O. Box 192
Waco, Ky. 40385
(606)369-5350
Handmade pottery.

MAINE

Basket Barn
Route 27 at River Road
Boothbay, Maine 04537
(207)633-5532
Contemporary baskets, country crafts,
pottery, quilt wall-hangings, and
ironware.

Howard G. Jones
24 Spear Street
Box 291
Rockport, Maine 04856
(207)236-4042
Nantucket Lightship baskets with
cherry bottoms, signed, dated, and
inscribed for owner.

Patchwork Barn
P.O. Box 326/Route 173
Lincolnville, Maine 08489
(207)763-3423
Rag rugs, raffia dolls, hook rugs,
bedspreads, patchwork quilts, and
country crafts.

Toby Soule & Susan Martens
Box 185
South Freeport, Maine 04078
(207)865-4855 or (207)688-2294
Colonial floorcloths, hand-stenciled
wall canvases, mirrors, stools, and
other furnishings.

Yankee Doodle
Sophia Gabriel & Kathy Hermann
132 Water Street
Hallowell, Maine 04347
(207)623-1526
Tinware, wrought iron, brass,
candles, linens, weather vanes, folk
art, salt-glaze pottery, baskets,
stenciled Shaker boxes, mirror frames,
and fabrics.

MARYLAND

Americana Marketplace
5000 Berwyn Road
College Park, Md. 20740
(301)474-2720
Contemporary folk art by artists
from many states.

Pine & Patches
5410 Olney-Laytonsville Road
Olney, Md. 20832
(301)948-5113
Tin ornaments, pottery, quilted
animals, and pillows.

Ram's Forge
2501 East Mayberry Road
Westminster, Md. 21157
(301)346-7873
Colonial and contemporary
wrought-iron work.

Cedar Swamp Stoneware Co., West Barnstable, Massachusetts

Still Ridge Herb Farm
10370 Route 99
Woodstock, Md. 21163
(301)465-8348
8129 Main Street
Ellicott City, Md. 21043
(301)461-9266
Wreaths, potpourri, sachets, seasonings,
tins, jars, pillows, and dried
Williamsburg flower arrangements.

MASSACHUSETTS

The Blacksmith Shop
RR 2/26 Bridge Road
Orleans, Mass. 02653
(617)255-7233
Museum-quality reproductions of
handwrought early American
ironware.

Brother Jonathan
Route 20/Box 415
Sturbridge, Mass. 01566
In Mass.: (617)347-7061
Outside Mass.: 1(800)343-0984
Country cupboards, quilts, folk art,
and handmade tin items.

Cedar Swamp Stoneware Co.
1645 Main Street
West Barnstable, Mass. 02668
(617)362-9906
Early American stoneware, including
limited editions, redware, and salt-
glazed stoneware. Catalog $1.

245

Karri McCue
404 Route 6A
East Sandwich, Mass. 02537
(617)888-6561
Primitive paintings.

Norton's Colonial Crafts
61 Water Street/P.O. Box 692
Newburyport, Mass. 01950
(617)462-9735
Birds, animals, and fish carved in
wood by a contemporary American folk
artist.

J. F. Orr & Sons
Village Green
Sudbury, Mass. 01776
(617)443-3650
New England country furniture,
handmade in 18th-century style:
country cupboards, dry sinks, and
tables made from hand-planed New
England white pine and cut nails, with
mortise-and-tenon joinery.

Restorations Studio 126 Inc.
Karen Matthews
118 Front Street
Marblehead, Mass. 01945
(617)631-6643
Pillows, quilts, and folk art by 45
contemporary artists.

Janet Russo
28 Main Street
Nantucket Island, Mass. 02554
(617)228-4818
Contemporary adaptations of antique
clothing, hand-knit sweaters, Victorian
linens, and quilts.

Salt & Chestnut
Route 6A at Maple Street
West Barnstable, Mass. 02668
(617)362-3012
Specializing in weather vanes.

Avis Skinner
Vis-a-Vis
Candle Street
Nantucket, Mass. 02554
(617)228-9102
Contemporary and antique clothing
and quilts, and one-of-a-kind Liberty
and Italian print cotton dresses and
skirts.

True Farm Antiques
68 True Road
Salisbury, Mass. 01950
(617)462-6296
Contemporary folk art: hand-carved
roosters, cats, watermelons, and fruit;
specializing in hand-carved shorebirds.

The Whippletree
Route 6A
West Barnstable, Mass. 02668
(617)362-3320
Dried herbs and plants, contemporary
folk art, and antiques.

MICHIGAN

American Country House
1063 South State
Davison, Mich. 48424
(313)653-0140
American primitive folk art and
country reproductions.

MISSOURI

Miniature Museum of Kansas City
Foundation
5235 Oak
Kansas City, Mo. 64110
(816)333-2055
A museum of antique dollhouses, with
a museum shop handling related items
and fine miniatures by contemporary
craftspeople.

Miniature Museum, Kansas City, Missouri

O'Dell House
466 South O'Dell
Marshall, Mo. 65340
(816)886-3663
Country antiques and contemporary
folk art, including silhouettes, hand-
painted pieces, stencils, whirligigs,
quilted and crocheted items, and floral
arrangements.

Ozark Mountain Collectables
Route 2/Box 126-C
Nixa, Mo. 65714
(417)725-3134
Wooden weather vanes, whirligigs,
and hand-painted American folk art.
Brochure available: $3.

Country Cousins, Charlotte, North Carolina

Radcliffe Antiques
Route 1/Box 139
Beaufort, Mo. 63013
(314)583-5898
Country furniture, folk art, bears,
and toys.

NEW JERSEY

The Bramble Patch
13 North Main Street
Mullica Hill, N.J. 08062
(609)478-6242
Folk art, rag rugs, quilts, weaving,
pottery, and other country accessories.

Keeping Room Antiques
69 East Main Street Rear
Moorestown, N.J. 08057
(609)234-0824
Specializing in contemporary
Pennsylvania fractur paintings;
country antiques and folk art by local
artists.

Those Were the Days
219 Lafayette Avenue
Hawthorne, N.J. 07506
(201)427-1054
Seat weaving, caning on premises;
caning supplies by mail order. Price
list: $1 with self-addressed stamped
envelope.

Well-Sweep Herb Farm
317 Mt. Bethel Road
Port Murray, N.J. 07865
(201)852-5390
Herb plants and dried flowers.

NEW YORK

Adirondack Craftmakers Cooperative,
Inc.
Route 28
Indian Lake, N.Y. 12842
(518)648-5130
Balsam and cedar sachets by 60
member craftspeople.

Lionel DeLong
Big Brook Road
Indian Lake, N.Y. 12842
(518)648-5566

Handmade log cabins in various styles
of completely natural materials—logs
kiln-dried, chinked with live moss,
no nails used; made to 1-inch-equals-
1-foot scale.

Mary Emmerling's American
Country Store
969 Lexington Avenue
New York, N.Y. 10021
(212)744-6705
and
Newman & Corwith
Bridgehampton, N.Y. 11932
(516)537-3408
Folk art and accessories by
contemporary artists, including
baskets, pottery, candles, tinwork,
quilted items, floorcloths, paintings,
weather vanes, whirligigs, and other
decorative pieces in tin or painted
wood displayed with American Country
antique furniture.

Ken Heitz
"Backwoods Furniture"
Box 161/Route 28
Indian Lake, N.Y. 12842
(518)251-3327
Rustic furniture from stools to beds.

247

Johnny Jupiter
385 Bleecker Street
New York, N.Y. 10014
and
884 Madison Avenue
New York, N.Y. 10021
(212)675-7574
Modern and antique folk art and
collectibles.

The Nelson Rockefeller Collection
11 East 57th Street
New York, N.Y. 10022
(212)581-0286
Folk art reproductions.

Erwin Rowland: Quilts &
Counterpanes
181 East 73rd Street
New York, N.Y. 10021
(212)249-1246
Ready-made and made-to-order quilts.
Color catalog available: $3.
By appointment only.

NORTH CAROLINA

The Betty Lamp, Ltd.
2318 Crescent Avenue
Charlotte, N.C. 28207
(704)375-6272
Contemporary American folk art and
handmade lighting.

J. B. Cole Pottery
P.O. Box 180
Sea Grove, N.C. 27341
(919)893-7171
Contemporary salt-glaze and slip
pottery.

Country Cousins
1121 McAlway Road
Charlotte, N.C. 28211
(704)364-6087
Antique and contemporary folk art;
grapevine wreaths.

Moravian Book & Gift Shop
614 South Main Street
Winston-Salem, N.C. 27101
(919)723-6262
Folk art, salt-glaze and slip pottery,
handmade tinware, hand-carved
wooden toys, and antique and
contemporary dolls.

Charles Spiron Decoy Company
Box 101/Highway 168
Currituck, N.C. 27929
(919)232-3227
Decoys, shorebirds, and folk art
carving.

Westmoore Pottery
Route 2/Box 159-A
Sea Grove, N.C. 27341
(919)464-3700
Cobalt decorated salt-glaze pottery and
slip-decorated redware; some
reproductions of old pieces.

OHIO

Jim Baker
P.O. Box 149
Worthington, Ohio 43085
(614)885-7040
Custom-designed fireboards, with oil on wood landscapes.

John Morgan Baker
P.O. Box 149
Worthington, Ohio 43085
(614)885-7040
Custom-made frames of curly maple for paintings, needlework, fractur. Mail-order service available.

Country Classics, The Shop on Main Street
9370 Main Street
Montgomery, Ohio 45242
(513)791-1335
Contemporary folk art, rag rugs, baskets, Old Sturbridge Village fabrics, wallpaper, and paints, stenciled muslin tab curtains; designs and builds reproduction country furniture.

The 1817 Shoppe
14659 E. Street/Route 37
Sunbury, Ohio 43074
(614)965-4392
Country reproduction furniture and accessories. Appointment and mail order.

Friendship Baskets
Marty Cates
P.O. Box 216
Lebanon, Ohio 45036
(513)932-2207
Handmade baskets. Brochure: $1. Minimum order: $150.

Sherman Hensal
P.O. Box 268
Lakemore, Ohio 44250
(216)894-8090
Folk art, including carved wooden vegetables, pies, and breads.

Elijah Pierce's Art Gallery
534 East Long Street
Columbus, Ohio 43215
(614)252-1559
Carved wood folk art.

Stone's Throw
6727 Lebanon Pike/Route 48
Springboro, Ohio 45066
(513)885-3300
Reproductions of folk art, 18th-century furniture, redware, and tin and copper lighting.

Warren County Historical Society
105 South Broadway
P.O. Box 223
Lebanon, Ohio 45036
(513)932-1817
Museum and gift shop—contemporary folk art.

Witter's Linden House
102 Linden Drive
Galion, Ohio 44833
(419)468-1956
Handmade baskets, natural wood and painted folk art, pillows, candles, dried and silk flower arrangements, tin, pewter, brass, ironware, Delft and Quimper.

PENNSYLVANIA

Tom Ahern Decoys
1017 Main Street
Hellertown, Pa. 18055
(215)838-7532
Wildlife art, specializing in hand-carved and painted bird sculpture.

George Arold
Shop Address:
Orvilla & School Roads
Hatfield, Pa. 19440
Mailing Address:
P.O. Box 99
Hatfield, Pa. 19440
(215)822-9630
Hand-dipped candles and candle-making supplies.

249

Basketry from Basket Road
Box 388 Basket Road/RD 1
Oley, Pa. 19547
(215)987-3734
Handmade baskets woven from local
willow, grapevine, honeysuckle, sea
grass, and rattan.

Breninger Taylor
Mansion Pottery
Taylor Mansion
476 South Church Street
Robesonia, Pa. 19551
(215)693-5344
Slipware, pottery, toys, sgraffito, and
plates.

Candy Americana Museum
46 North Broad Street
Lititz, Pa. 17543
Handmade folk art; candy.

The Dilworthtown Country Store
275 Brintons Bridge Road
West Chester, Pa. 19380
(215)399-0560
Folk art.

Morgan L. Dively
Hickory Rocking Chairs
Polecat Hollow Road/RD 1/Box 567
East Freedom, Pa. 16637
(814)239-5882
Chair maker.

Thomas G. Loose
RD 2/Box 124
Leesport, Pa. 19533
(215)926-4849
Blacksmith, whitesmith, handwrought
iron items for hearth and home. Mail
order available.

Pennsylvania Firebacks
Hearth and Home Catalogue
1011 East Washington Lane
Philadelphia, Pa. 19138
(215)843-6162
Handmade American craft items and
fireplace accessories, including
fireboards and firebacks.

Raintree Gallery Folk Art Carvers
B. Leader, Wood-carver–Designer
204 North Poplar Street
Elizabethtown, Pa. 17022
(717)367-2990
Hand-carved two- and three-
dimensional folk art pieces by a group
of 10 carvers.

Sawtooth Folk Art
6 Marion Court
Lancaster, Pa. 17602
(717)393-3884
Contemporary folk art, specializing in
Amish quilts, baskets, primitive
paintings, and rag rugs.

John Wright Factory Store
North Front Street/Box C 40
Wrightsville, Pa. 17368
(717)252-2519
Manufacturer of cast-iron
reproductions, many made from the
original molds.

TEXAS

Great Expectations Quilts Inc.
155 Town & Country Village
Houston, Tex. 77024
(713)465-7622
Contemporary quilts, reproduction
and country fabrics, and handmade
baskets.

Ouisie's Storeside
1724 Sunset Boulevard
Houston, Tex. 77005
(713)527-9125
Ethnic jewelry, potpourri, frames, and
decorative pieces.

The Quilt Collector
2034 West Gray
Houston, Tex. 77019
(713)524-8281
Contemporary quilts, American folk
art, and American Country accessories.

VERMONT

Ian Eddy, Blacksmith
RFD 1/Sand Hill Road
Putney, Vt. 05346
(802)387-5991
Handwrought objects, including
utensil racks, fireplace and wood-stove
tools, plant hangers, and lighting
fixtures.

The Store at Sugarbush Village
Route 100/Box 118
Waitsfield, Vt. 05673
(802)583-2288 or (802)496-4465
Country collectibles.

VIRGINIA

The Dower Chest, Ltd.
1206 Jamestown Road
Williamsburg, Va. 23185
(804)229-8527
Contemporary folk art, primitive
paintings, twig and honeysuckle
baskets, and quilted accessories.

Fredericksburg Pottery
800 Sophia Street
Fredericksburg, Va. 22401
(703)371-1730
Production pottery workshop and
retail showroom open to the public.

Paula Lewis Court Square
Fourth & East Jefferson
Charlottesville, Va. 22901
(804)295-6244
Specializing in quilts.

Persnickety
Village Centre
776 East Walker Road
Great Falls, Va. 22066
(703)759-3880
Contemporary folk art, furniture, and
accessories.

The Very Thing
On the Green at the Boar's Head
Charlottesville, Va. 22901
(804)296-8379
Handcrafted gifts and clothing.

Yorktown Creative Art Center
"On the Hill"
Alexander Hamilton Boulevard at
Ballard Street
Yorktown, Va. 23690
(804)898-3076
A cooperative of 45 participating
artists who display and sell their work.

WASHINGTON, D.C.

Liberty
Cornelia Wickens
1513 Wisconsin Avenue N.W.
Washington, D.C. 20007
(202)337-5742
One-of-a-kind Victorian blouses and
hand-knitted sweaters; antique and
new Victorian nightgowns, linens, and
quilts; pillows, skirts, toys, and
ornaments made from antique quilts.

WEST VIRGINIA

Yesteryear Toy Co.
P.O. Box 3283
Charleston, W. Va. 25332
(304)744-2162
Hand-painted wooden toys.

Directory

OF ANTIQUES DEALERS

The "Directory of Antiques Dealers" lists 280 dealers throughout the United States who specialize in American Country antiques. This is a completely new listing of dealers not included in *American Country* and should be used as a companion to the directory in the first book. Many dealers are available by appointment only, so it is advisable to call before you visit. Check with local dealers for directories of other dealers in the area.

ARKANSAS

The Sassafras Shop
1003 Park Avenue
Hot Springs, Ark. 71901
(501)623-7261

CALIFORNIA

Bale Mill Antiques
3431 North St. Helena Highway
St. Helena, Calif. 94574
(707)963-4545

Bayberry Antiques
953 North Van Ness
Fresno, Calif. 93728
(209)485-0691

Blue Quail Antiques
31531 Camino Capistrano
San Juan, Calif. 92675
(714)661-5709

The Carousel Antiques &
Country Store
312 & 316 Sir Frances Drake
Boulevard
San Anselmo, Calif. 94960
Main Store: (415)453-6373
Country Store: (415)457-5141

253

Margaret Cavigga
8648 Melrose Avenue
Los Angeles, Calif. 90069
(213)659-3020

Celebrated Works
8443 Melrose Avenue
Los Angeles, Calif. 90069
(213)658-7850

Clark's Corner Antiques
1333 West Washington Boulevard
Venice, Calif. 90291
(213)396-6217 or (213)645-8789

Country Corner Antiques
4904 Soquel Drive
Soquel, Calif. 95073
(408)462-5188

Kiracofe and Kile, San Francisco

Kiracofe and Kile
955 Fourteenth Street
San Francisco, Calif. 94114
(415)431-1222
By appointment only.

Richard Mulligan Antiques
8471 Melrose Avenue
Los Angeles, Calif. 90069
(213)653-0204

Nonesuch Gallery, Santa Monica, California

Nonesuch Gallery
1211 Montana Avenue
Santa Monica, Calif. 90403
(213)393–1245

Parrish & Sons Antiques
508 Brinkerhoff Avenue
Santa Barbara, Calif. 93101
(805)962-6005

The Pavillion Antiques
610 Sir Frances Drake Boulevard
San Anselmo, Calif. 94960
(415)459-2002

Pilgrim/Roy
372 Hayes Street
San Francisco, Calif. 94102
(415)431-9521
and
5821 College Avenue
Oakland, Calif. 94618
(415)655-6933

Plum Pudding
Carole and Jim Burnis
P.O. Box 160664
Sacramento, Calif. 95816
(916)455-0768

Margaret Cavigga, Los Angeles, California

"Something Else" Antiques
13101 East Whittier Boulevard
Whittier, Calif. 90602
(213)693-6614

The Three Witches Antiques
2843 California Street
San Francisco, Calif. 94115
(415)922-0940

Thru the Barn Door
6526 Washington Street
Yountville, Calif. 94599
(707)944-2644

COLORADO

James Brooks' Magnificent Obsession
31 South 80th Street
Boulder, Colo. 80303
(303)499-7009

CONNECTICUT

James Bok Antiques
1954 Post Road
Fairfield, Conn. 06430
(203)255-6500

Holly Meier, Norfolk, Connecticut

The Family Album
283 Post Road East
Westport, Conn. 06880
(203)227-4888

Suzanne Feldman
Route 112 West
Lakeville, Conn. 06039
(203)435-2674

Pat Field
79 Norfield Road
Weston, Conn. 06883
(203)226-9983

Nancy Fierberg Antiques
107 Main Street North
Woodbury, Conn. 06798
(203)263-4957

Pat Guthman Antiques
342 Pequot
Southport, Conn.
(203)259-5743

Marilyn Dozier Hoak
410 Albany Turnpike
Canton, Conn. 06019
(203)693-2732

Holly Meier
The Old Farm
Colebrook Road
Norfolk, Conn. 06058
(203)542-5380

Norma's Antiques
Turnpike Road
Somers, Conn. 06071
(203)749-0324

Suzy and Carol's Antiques
Canon Crossing
Wilton, Conn. 06897
(203)762-3004

Ten Eyck—Emerich
351 Pequot Avenue
Southport, Conn. 06490
(203)259-2559

DELAWARE

The Yankee Smuggler
402 Delaware Avenue
McDaniel Crest
Wilmington, Del. 19803
(302)478-2681
By appointment only.

GEORGIA

The Antique Store of Marietta
81 Church Street
Marietta, Ga. 30060
(404)428-3376

June Harrison Antiques, Charlotte, North Carolina

Back Porch Antiques
5488 Peachtree Road
Chamblee, Ga. 30341
(404)458-1614

Mountain City Antiques
P.O. Box 305/Highway 441
Mountain City, Ga. 30562
(404)746-2320 or (404)746-2298

The Mulberry Tree
205 West River Street
Savannah, Ga. 31401
(912)236-4656

IDAHO

Cobweb Antiques
915 Powerline
Nampa, Idaho 83651
(208)466-3068

The Hissing Goose
P.O. Box 597
Fourth and Leadville
Ketchum, Idaho 83340
(208)726-3036

ILLINOIS

Diane Elliott
1 Hill Street
Galena, Ill. 61036
(815)777-0694

The Flower Mill
Country Furniture
17 West 406 22nd Street
Oakbrook Terrace, Ill. 60181
(312)832-2889

Hammer & Hammer
American Folk Art
620 North Michigan Avenue,
Suite 470
Chicago, Ill. 60611
(312)266-8512

Barbara A. Johnson
Clock Tower Inn
7801 East State Street
Rockford, Ill. 61125
(815)397-6699

Saltbox Antiques
1017 E. Adams
Washington, Ill. 61571
(309)444-2335
By appointment only.

INDIANA

Jane and Henry Eckert
900 East Main
Westfield, Ind. 46074
(317)896-3081

Carol Swope's Americana
3828 Payne Koehler Road
New Albany, Ind. 47150
(812)948-1491

Wolf's Den
Rural Route 8
Bair Road
Columbia City, Ind. 46725
(219)691-3592

Ginni and Bud Zink
301 Chipaway Drive
Alexandria, Ind. 46001
(317)724-4629

KANSAS

Smith House
3304 West Sixth
Topeka, Kan. 66606
(913)357-0709

Virginia's Antiques
West Fifth Street
Hoyt, Kan. 66440
(913)986-6540

KENTUCKY

Boone Trace Antiques
335 Bacon Court
Harrodsburg, Ky. 40330
(606)734-2657

Wooden Spoon Antiques
2724 Frankfort Avenue
Louisville, Ky. 40206

LOUISIANA

Avondale Plantation
P.O. Box 8187
Highway 10 East
Clinton, La. 70722
(504)683-5004

Doris Stauble, Wiscasset, Maine

Serendipity
3846 Government
Baton Rouge, La. 70806
(504)389-0055

MAINE

Apex Antiques
98 High Street
Belfast, Maine 04915
(207)338-1194

The Captain Jefferds Inn
Pearl Street/Box 691
Kennebunkport, Maine 04046
(207)967-2311

The Emporium
47 Middle Street
Portland, Maine 04101
(207)773-2648

Captain Jefferds Inn, Kennebunkport, Maine

English Meadows Inn
RFD 1/Route 35
Lower Village
Kennebunkport, Maine 04046
(207)967-5766

Forbes Antiques
Shop Location:
Main Street
Wiscasset, Maine 04578
Mailing Address:
P.O. Box 331
Wiscasset, Maine 04578
(207)882-6351

Dale and Gary Guyette
Antiques
Box 522
West Farmington, Maine 04992
(207)778-6266

Lilac Cottage Antiques
On The Green
Wiscasset, Maine 04578
(207)882-7059

Marine Antiques
Route 1
Wiscasset, Maine 04578
(207)882-7208

Mt. Vernon Antiques
Box 248
Mt. Vernon, Maine 04352
(207)293-2397

Newcastle Antiques
Route 1
Newcastle, Maine 04553
(207)563-5714 or (207)586-5631

Margaret Brockway Ofslager
Route 1
Wiscasset, Maine 04578
(207)882-6082

The Old Barn
Annex Antiques
RFD 2/Gurnet Road
Brunswick, Maine 04011
(207)729-8975

The Porringer
Water Street
Wiscasset, Maine 04578
(207)882-7951

Reynolds & Marcus Antiques
Old Barn Annex 2
Middle Street
Wiscasset, Maine 04578
(207)882-6768

Schneider's Antiques
130 Water Street
Hallowell, Maine 04347
(207)622-0002

Doris Stauble
Summer Street
Wiscasset, Maine 04578
(207)882-5286

Pat Stauble
P.O. Box 265
Wiscasset, Maine 04578
(207)882-5286

The Tin Feather
Coastal Route 1 South
Kennebunk, Maine 04043
(207)985-6279

Townsend Place Antiques
Gleason Hill   Box 946
Union, Maine 04862
(207)785-2462

Vintage Antiques
84–88 Middle Street
Portland, Maine 04101
(207)775-1600

MARYLAND

Dickeyville Gallery
2412 Pickwick Road
Baltimore, Md. 21207
(301)448-0063

Marshland Primitives
412 Spring Creek Road
Hagerstown, Md. 21740
(301)790-1245 or (301)790-2666

Bettie Mintz, Bethesda, Maryland

Avis Skinner/Vis-a-Vis, Nantucket, Massachusetts

Bettie Mintz
P.O. Box 5943
Bethesda, Md. 20014
(301)652-4626

John C. Newcomer
Route 1
Box 35A
Keedysville, Md. 21756
(301)790-1327

Pack Rats
400 Greenbrier Drive
Silver Spring, Md. 20910
(301)565-9325

MASSACHUSETTS

J. T. Browne Antiques
P.O. Box 109
Hampden, Mass. 01036
(413)566-8488

Folk Art Antiques
Snug Harbor
Duxbury, Mass. 02332

The Gallery of Folk Art
170 Washington Street
Marblehead, Mass. 01945
(617)631-1594

Island Attic Industries
99 Washington Street
Nantucket, Mass. 02554
and
Miacomet Avenue
Nantucket, Mass. 02554
(617)228-9405

Mona S. Janelle
514 Center Street
Rural Route 2
Dennisport, Mass. 02639
(617)394-2791

Paul Madden Antiques
5 North Water Street
Nantucket, Mass. 02554
(617)228-0112

Maynard House Antiques
11 Maynard Street
Westborough, Mass. 01581
(617)366-2073

Paul Madden Antiques, Nantucket, Massachusetts

Nantucket House Antiques
8 Fair Street
Nantucket Island, Mass. 02554
(617)228-4604

Nantucket Trading Co., Ltd.
1 South Beach Street
Nantucket, Mass. 02554
(617)228-3221

257

Jo-Ann E. Ross
1679 Somerset Avenue
Taunton, Mass. 02780
(617)824-8255

Shady Lady Antiques
Route 28 at Lilly Pulitzer
Orleans, Mass. 02643
(617)255-8735

Avis Skinner
Vis-a-Vis
Candle Street
Nantucket, Mass. 02554
(617)228-9102

Sunsmith House Antiques
Route 6-A
Brewster, Cape Cod, Mass. 02631
(617)896-7024

Dianne Vetromile
379 Commercial
Provincetown, Mass. 02657
(617)487-3522

Lynda Willauer
2 India Street
Nantucket, Mass. 02554
(617)228-3631
May through September.

Yellow Barn Antiques
11 Barnes Road
Newton, Mass. 02158
(617)527-0518
By appointment only.

MICHIGAN

American Horse Antiques
and Folk Art
25009 Chambley
Southfield, Mich. 48034
(313)352-5995 or (313)352-5959

Country Store Antiques
196 West Liberty
Plymouth, Mich. 48170
(313)459-9850

Culpepper's Quilts
210 Abbott
East Lansing, Mich. 48823
(517)332-2927

Sandra Mitchell
25009 Chambley
Southfield, Mich. 48034
(313)352-5995
By appointment only.

Eric and Carol Nordell
Folk Art and Quilts
15746 Bradner Road
Northville, Mich. 48167
(313)420-3237

Sign of the Windsor Chair
4472 Greenstown Drive
Orchard Lake, Mich. 48033
(313)681-9443
By appointment only.

MINNESOTA

American Classics Antiques
Jeffrey Drogue, Marge Drogue, and
Kerrie Drogue Anderson
4944 Xerxes Avenue South
Minneapolis, Minn. 55410
(612)926-2509

MISSISSIPPI

Irma Felts Antiques
1763 South Market Street
Pascagoula, Miss. 39567
(601)769-6401

The Kausler House
Antiques—Interiors
Circa 1875
737 North President Street
Jackson, Miss. 39202
(601)353-1038

Green Willow Farm Antiques, Greenwood, Missouri

MISSOURI

American System Antiques
Westphalia, Mo. 65085
(314)455-2525
By appointment only.

Barwood Farm Antiques
Rural Route 1
Columbia, Mo. 65201
(314)449-3051

Boone's Lick Trail Antiques
4038 East Broadway
Columbia, Mo. 65201
(314)442-6759

Cornucopia Antiques
Sue Williams
Route 1   Thompson, Mo. 65285
(314)682-3841

Countryside Antiques
Rural Route 1
Laddonia, Mo. 63352
(314)249-5744

Gardner Company
Folk Art Collection
P.O. Box 1087
West Highway 76
Branson, Mo. 65616
(417)334-8089

Green Willow Farm Antiques
Greenwood, Mo. 64034
(816)537-6527

Hope Antiques
Box 127/Route 1
Morrison, Mo. 65061
(314)943-6694

Keeping Room Antiques at
Rock Evan Farm
Route #2
Russellville, Mo. 65074

Maple Hill Farm Antiques
P.O. Box 68
Labadie, Mo. 63055
(314)742-4333

Meetinghouse Antiques
Route 1/Box 135
Labadie, Mo. 63055
(314)742-3400

Old Stone House Antiques
200 Franklin Street
Hermann, Mo. 65041
(314)486-2000

Oldetyme Antiques
Faye Ward Anderson,
Charles S. Anderson III
1811–13 West 45th
Kansas City, Mo. 64111
(816)531-6824

Patchwork Sampler
9735 Clayton Road
St. Louis, Mo. 63124
(314)997-6116

Robinwood Farm Antiques
Route 1/Box 305
Moberly, Mo. 65270
(816)263-6507

Richard Saunders Antiques
Box 56
Rocheport, Mo. 65279
(314)698-3765

The Smith Co.
4444 Bell Street
Kansas City, Mo. 64111
(816)931-5234

Stark
1714 West 45th
Kansas City, Mo. 64111
(816)561-1842

The Summer Kitchen
Route 1/Box 112
New Haven, Mo. 63068
(314)459-6542

Toy Box Antiques
401 East Highway "N"
Wentzville, Mo. 63385
(314)327-8089

Melissa Williams
Antiques at Greenwood
2810 Paris Road
Columbia, Mo. 65202
(314)474-6515

Wooden Horse Antiques
Route 1/Box 187
Boles Road
Labadie, Mo. 63055
(314)742-2293

NEBRASKA

Raggedy Ann's Antique &
Gift Shoppe

1527 North Cotner Boulevard
Lincoln, Neb. 68505
(402)464-0456

NEW HAMPSHIRE

Hayseed Antiques
Route 130 West/523 Broad Street
Nashua, N.H. 03063
(603)889-9731

Hoffman's
1780 Cape Antiques
Box 434/RD 2

Laconia, N.H. 03246
(603)528-2792

NEW JERSEY

Bari and Phil Axelband
109 Wood Terrace
Leonia, N.J. 07605
(201)461-8467

The Country Goose
Geri and Bruce Shenk
West Caldwell, N.J. 07006
(201)228-4923
By appointment only.

Cricket Creek Antiques
Guinea Hollow Road
Mountainville, N.J. 08833
(201)832-2882

Denison Ridge Antiques
Box 567
Saddle River, N.J. 07458
(201)327-9249 or (201)327-3137

Eagles Nest Antiques
38 South Main Street
Mullica Hill, N.J. 08062
(609)478-6351

259

Sandra E. Gilenta
P.O. Box 405
Manasquan, N.J. 08736
(201)528-8546

Grey Cat Antiques
54 South Main Street
Mullica Hill, N.J. 08062
(609)423-5211
By appointment only.

King's Row (7 Dealers)
44 North Main Street
Mullica Hill, N.J. 08062
(609)478-4361

Lafayette Mill Market (40 Dealers)
Route 15 and Meadows Road
Lafayette, N.J. 07848
(201)383-9032 or (201)383-0065

Kate & Stan Lamborne Antiques
36 South Main Street
Mullica Hill, N.J. 08062
(609)478-2484

Linenworks Etc.
at Antiques & Uniques
32 Willow Drive
Little Silver, N.J. 07739
(201)741-2728

Bob Lutz Antiques
Main Street/Route 29
Stockton, N.J. 08559
(609)397-3398

Susan Maffei/American
Country Antiques
RD 1/Box 150 B
Matawan, N.J. 07747
(201)566-4903
By appointment only.

Mail Pouch Antiques
Water Street

Mountainville, N.J. 08833
(201)832-7194

Oltz/Regner
RD/Anderson Road
Clinton, N.J. 08809
(201)638-8630
204 Lafayette Avenue
Chatham, N.J. 07928
(201)635-2037
By appointment only.

Patricia of Mullica Hill
99 North Main Street
Mullica Hill, N.J. 08062
(609)478-4737

Carole Pegoraro
Fox Run/RR 3
Tewksbury Township
Califon, N.J. 07830
(201)832-7930

Swamp Mill Farm Antiques
109 West Saddle River Road
Saddle River, N.J. 07458
Mailing Address:
P.O. Box 402
Saddle River, N.J. 07458
(201)327-6252

Hedy Schwind Antiques
RD 5/Box 211
Flemington, N.J. 08822
(201)782-8340

Village Antiques
Main Street Mountainville
RD 2
Lebanon, N.J. 08833
(201)832-2227

Mary and Charles Weinman
P.O. Box 274
Cedar Grove, N.J. 07009
(201)239-0939

Whirligig Antiques
Ellen Katona and Bette Phillips
RD 2/Box 288
Stockton, N.J. 08559
(201)996-6854

NEW MEXICO

Circa
555 Canyon Road
Santa Fe, N. Mex. 87501
(505)983-9797

Forest Fenn, Sante Fe, New Mexico

Forest Fenn
1075 Paseo de Perlata
Sante Fe, N. Mex. 87501
(505)982-4631

The Santa Fe Co.
419 Canyon Road
Santa Fe, N. Mex. 87501
(505)983-4094

NEW YORK

America Hurrah Antiques
766 Madison Avenue
New York, N.Y. 10021
(212)535-1930

American Primitive
242 West 30th Street
5th floor
New York, N.Y. 10003
(212)239-1345

The American Wing
Box 1131 Montauk Highway
Bridgehampton, N.Y. 11932
(516)537-3319

Ruth Bigel Antiques
743 Madison Avenue
New York, N.Y. 10021
(212)988-3116

The Bird's Nest Antiques
Trinity Pass in Scotts Corners
Pound Ridge, N.Y. 10567
(914)764-8323

The Blue Door Antiques
Montauk Highway
Bridgehampton, N.Y. 11932
(516)537-1155

America Hurrah Antiques, New York City

C & P Antique Pickers
8 Mills Pond Road
St. James, N.Y. 11780
(516)862-6145

Audree & Bryce Chase's
Collector Corner
62 Main Street
East Bloomfield, N.Y. 14443
(716)657-6227

Leslie Eisenberg Folk Art Gallery
820 Madison Avenue
New York, N.Y. 10021
(212)628-5454

*Mary Emmerling's American Country Store,
Bridgehampton, New York*

Mary Emmerling's American
Country Store
969 Lexington Avenue
New York, N.Y. 10021
(212)744-6705
and
Newman & Corwith
Bridgehampton, N.Y. 11932
(516)537-3408

Laura Fisher
1050 Second Avenue
Gallery #73
New York, N.Y. 10022
Business: (212)838-2596
Evening: (212)866-6033

Goose Cove Antiques
118 Main Street
Tappan, N.Y. 10983
(914)359-9433

Evan G. Hughes, Inc.
522 Third Avenue
New York, N.Y. 10016
(212)MU 3-2441
and
390 Bleecker Street
New York, N.Y. 10014
(212)691-9418

The Incurable Collector Antiques
Bridge Street
Schoharie, N.Y. 12157
(518)295-7434

Jenkinstown Antiques
520 Route 32 South
New Paltz, N.Y. 12561
(914)255-8135

Kenos Antiques
RD 1/Box 391
Mohawk, N.Y. 13407
(315)866-1055

Lane's End
Ridge Road
Natural Bridge, N.Y. 13665
(315)644-4097

Made in America Country
Antiques & Quilts
1234 Madison Avenue
New York, N.Y. 10028
(212)289-1113

Marlene
185 East 79th Street
New York, N.Y. 10021
(212)737-7671

Morgan MacWhinnie
520 North Sea Road
Southampton, N.Y. 11968
(516)283-3366

Morgan MacWhinnie, Southampton, New York

Pear Tree Antiques
P.O. Box 1832
Sag Harbor, N.Y. 11963
(516)725-4055

Mary Emmerling's American Country Store, New York City

Gene Reed Country Antiques—
Contemporary Folk Art
75 South Broadway
Nyack, N.Y. 10960
(914)358-3750

Ricco-Johnson Gallery
475 Broome Street
New York, N.Y. 10013
(212)966-0541

Sage Street Antiques
Box 504
Sag Harbor, N.Y. 11963
(516)725-4036

Kathy Schoemer Antiques
Trinity Pass & Westchester Avenue
Scotts Corners
Pound Ridge, N.Y. 10576
(914)764-5688

Marianne Smullin
New City, N.Y.
(914)634-5258
By appointment only.

Spirit of America
269 West 4th Street
New York, N.Y. 10014
(212)255-3255

Eliza Werner
Main Street
Bridgehampton, N.Y. 11932
(516)725-4036

White Horse Antiques
Montauk Highway
Quogue, N.Y. 11959
(516)653-4946
Open Summers.
Off Season: Weekends or
by appointment.

NORTH CAROLINA

Da'Ka Antiques
208 North Mendenhall Street
Greensboro, N.C. 27401
(919)273-2312

Harry Davis
P.O. Box 215
Sanford, N.C. 27330
(919)776-3553

Griffin's Antiques
Route 7/Box 958
Greensboro, N.C. 27407
(919)454-3362

June Harrison Antiques
2250 Colony Road
Charlotte, N.C. 28209
(704)375-4104

Kildaire Barn Antiques (11 Dealers)
1401 Kildaire Farm Road
Cary, N.C. 27511
(919)469-1488

Willow Oak Antiques, Lexington, North Carolina

Matthews Emporium
P.O. Box 1006
Matthews, N.C. 28105
(704)847-6624

*Southern Keeping Room,
Charlotte, North Carolina*

Southern Keeping Room
Hannelis Kuntze
1721 Fountain View
Charlotte, N.C. 28203
(704)335-0686

June Harrison Antiques, Charlotte, North Carolina

Southern Manner
Linda and Tom Beatty,
Wayne W. Haigler
106 North Trade Street
P.O. Box 1706
Matthews, N.C. 28105
(704)847-3698

Willis Stallings
125 Cloverleaf, N.W.
High Point, N.C. 27260
(919)882-1124

Willow Oak Antiques
Route 12/Highway 52
Lexington, N.C. 27292
(919)764-0192

OHIO

Baker's Antiques of Washington
Square
Box 375
Waynesville, Ohio 45068
(513)298-2077

Virginia Bare Antiques
11885 U.S. Route 50
Hillsboro, Ohio 45133
(513)365-1223

The Barnabas Crane House
William L. Hromy
5958 Ridge Road (SR 94)
Wadsworth, Ohio 44281
(216)239-1409

The Butter Churn
Sue Potchen
106 Olive Street
Chagrin Falls, Ohio 44022
(216)247-5310

Joan R. Coulter Antiques
123 Center Street/P.O. Box 356
Milan, Ohio 44846
(419)499-4061

Betty Murray, Canal Winchester, Ohio

Country Weeds & Things
9414 Township Road 249
Galion, Ohio 44833
(419)362-4125

J. W. Lingo Antiques, Lebanon, Ohio

Cranmer's
Sharon Center Antiques
Box 274
Sharon Center, Ohio 44274
(216)239-1525

Joan Darnall
3693 Yellow Creek Road
Akron, Ohio 44313
(216)666-4827

Delagrange
12 North High Street
Jeromesville, Ohio 44840
(419)368-8971

East Liberty Antiques
536 East Liberty Street
Medina, Ohio 44256
(216)725-0678

Griffin's Antiques, Greensboro, North Carolina

Elderly Things
16970 Auburn Road
Chagrin Falls, Ohio 44022
(216)543-8689

Federation Antiques, Inc.
2700 Observatory (at Edwards)
Cincinnati, Ohio 45208
(513)321-2671

Four Chimneys Antiques
172 East U.S. 22–3
Maineville, Ohio 45039
(513)683-6486

Garth's Auctions, Inc.
P.O. Box 369
Delaware, Ohio 43015
(614)362-4771
Auctions only.

Pat Gesler Antiques
2129 Stancrest Road
Dublin, Ohio 43017
(614)889-0232

Sheila Gorman American
Country Antiques
P.O. Box 331/Route 45
Austinburg, Ohio 44010
(216)275-3891

263

The Herb Basket
P.O. Box 295/777 Hatch Road
Sharon Center, Ohio 44274
(216)239-2373

Ruth Keneda Antiques
3186 Stony Hill Road
Medina, Ohio 44256
(216)239-2571

Knapp and Farley Antiques
135 Boston Mills Road
Boston Heights, Hudson, Ohio 44236
(216)653-6141

J. W. Lingo Antiques
3 South Broadway
Lebanon, Ohio 45036
(513)932-0269

Ray and Kathy Mongenas
600 Hanna
Loveland, Ohio 45140
(513)683-8888

Betty Murray
37 Liberty
Canal Winchester, Ohio 43110
(614)837-6307
By appointment only.

Nine Lives Antiques
P.O. Box 403/77 South Main Street
Waynesville, Ohio 45068
(513)897-7455

Delagrange, Jeromesville, Ohio

Plain & Simple
691 Park Avenue
Cincinnati, Ohio 45246
(513)825-9484

S & A Americana
8822 Turin Hill South
Dublin, Ohio 43017
(614)764-9339

Salt Box House Antiques
16 South Main Street
Milan, Ohio 44846
(419)499-4201

The Salt Box in Ghent
858 Wye Road
Akron, Ohio 44313
(216)666-8539

Marjorie Staufer, Medina, Ohio

Second Time Around Toys &
Primitives
c/o Iron Fence Interiors
344 North Market Street
Galion, Ohio 44833
(419)468-5239

Sign of the Goose
223 Green Street
Dayton, Ohio 45402
(513)222-5166
By chance or appointment.

Smoke Rise Acres Antiques
Ted and Nancy Bossford
8 East 5th Street/P.O. Box #51
The Plains, Ohio 45780
(614)797-4456

Marjorie Staufer
2244 Remsen Road
Medina, Ohio 44256
(216)239-1443

Stone Eagle Farm
Avon, Ohio 44011
(216)937-6461 or (216)936-6561
By appointment only.

Strawberry Hill Antiques
3066 Stony Hill Road
Medina, Ohio 44256
(216)239-2400

Joan K. Townsend
4215 Utica Road
Lebanon, Ohio 45036
(513)932-3619
By appointment only.

Wanna Buy a Duck
805 McKinley N.W.
Canton, Ohio 44703
(216)493-0451

Wren Cottage Antiques
2125 Kellogg Road
Hinckley, Ohio 44233
(216)278-4895

Four Chimneys Antiques, Maineville, Ohio

OKLAHOMA

Colonial Antiques
1325 East 15th
Tulsa, Okla. 74120
3747 South Peoria
Tulsa, Okla. 74105
(918)585-3865

The Orange Crate
2548 NW 12th
Oklahoma City, Okla. 73107
(405)524-4328

OREGON

Grandma's Cellar
715 Sunset Drive
Ontario, Ore. 97914
(503)889-8591

PENNSYLVANIA

Robert J. Anderson Folk Art
Pa. Star Route/Box 16
Upper Black Eddy, Pa. 18972
(215)294-9441

Robert J. Anderson Folk Art
(second location)
16 Race Street
Frenchtown, N.J. 08825
(201)996-3344

Bea Cohen Antiques
Box 825
Easton, Pa. 18042
(215)252-1098
By appointment only.

Country Antiques at the Church
Route 202 & Upper Mountain Road
RD 1/Box 58 A
New Hope, Pa. 18938
(215)794-5009

America Hurrah Antiques, New York City

Coventry Antiques
RD 2/Olde Route 23
Coventryville, Pa. 19464
(215)469-9179

The Cunninghams
P.O. Box 142
Denver, Pa. 17517
(215)267-2981

The Dilworthtown Country Store
275 Brintons Bridge Road
West Chester, Pa. 19380
(215)399-0560

Grant Street
126 East Grant Street
Lancaster, Pa. 17602
(717)397-8130

Fae B. Haight Antiques
Lahaska Antique Court
P.O. Box 294/Route 202
Lahaska, Pa. 18931
Business: (215)794-7884
Home: (215)348-2442

Rosemary Jones Antiques
River Road
New Hope, Pa. 18938
(215)862-2195

Secret Cupboard Antiques
234 East Market Street
Marietta, Pa. 17547
(717)426-2412

Steckel House Antiques
Northampton & Chestnut Streets
Bath, Pa. 18014
(215)837-7766

Stone's Antiques
RD 1/Box 388
Zionsville, Pa. 18092
(215)679-2325

Toad Hall Antiques
Route 23/RD 4
Pottstown, Pa. 19464
(215)469-9471

Nan and Jim Tshudy
Ephrata, Lang Co.
Box 224/RD 4
Ephrata, Pa. 17522
(717)733-2175

Scott Tyson
Route 23/Box 116
Lancaster County,
Goodville, Pa. 17528
(215)445-7676

RHODE ISLAND

Lida Gerritsen
Wildwood Farm
Lawton Foster Road
Hopkinton, R.I. 02833
(401)377-2695

SOUTH CAROLINA

Brick Kitchen Antiques
21 Wentworth Street
Anson Borough
Charleston, S.C. 29401
(803)577-4944

TENNESSEE

The Country Sampler
107 South Kilgore Street
Athens, Tenn. 37303
(615)745-6912 or
(615)745-8010

Eloise Jeffries Antiques
1101 Otter Creek Road
Nashville, Tenn. 37220
(615)832-1611

Old Log Cabin Antiques
1720 East Spring Street
Cookeville, Tenn. 38501
(615)526-2306

Bob and Donna Parrott
433 Scenic Drive
Knoxville, Tenn. 37919
(615)525-6359

Quilter's Haven
P.O. Box 151/Wartrace Road
Bell Buckle, Tenn. 37020
(615)389-9292

Trace Tavern Antiques
8456 Highway 100
Nashville, Tenn. 37221
(615)646-5600

The Walnut Tree Antiques
Jack and Wilma Murray
11529 Nassau Drive
Knoxville, Tenn. 37922
(615)966-9028

TEXAS

Balene, Inc.
2005D West Gray
Houston, Tex. 77019
(713)523-2304

Robert E. Kinnaman and Brian Ramaekers, Houston, Texas

Gingerbread House Antiques
17811 Bramwood
Houston, Tex. 77090
(713)444-6452
By appointment only.

The Gypsy Savage
1507 Indiana
Houston, Tex. 77006
(713)528-0897

Heart of Country Antiques
210 East Chambers
Cleburne, Tex. 76031
(817)645-9568 (Burnett)
(817)641-6854 (Barr)

Kay Humphreys and
Annell Livingston
401 Byron Nelson Drive
McAllen, Tex. 78501
(512)687-4192
10007 Briar Drive
Houston, Tex. 77042
(713)783-1838
By appointment and Shows.

Jabberwocky
310 East Main
Fredericksburg, Tex. 78624
(512)997-7071

Frankie Mae Jenkins
Lone Star Quilters
101 Lake Street at College Avenue
Bryan, Tex. 77801
(713)775-8953

Robert E. Kinnaman and
Brian Ramaekers
River Oaks Center at
2002 Peden Street
Houston, Tex. 77019
(713)526-0095

The Painted Parson
1300 South Broadway
Carrollton, Tex. 75006
(214) 242-3113

Verities & Balderdash
102 West Alabama Street
Wharton, Tex. 77488
(713)532-5325

Joan M. Wilson
301 Top Hill Drive
Tyler, Tex. 75703
(214)561-0474

The Wooden Star Antiques
4368 Westheimer on Mid Lane
Houston, Tex. 77027
(713)629-1892

June Worrell
502 Welch
Houston, Tex. 77006
(713)524-0071

VERMONT

L. T. Hall, Antiques and Quilts
26 Central Street
Woodstock, Vt. 05091
(802)457-3360

VIRGINIA

Antique Court of Shoppes
104–106 William Street
Fredericksburg, Va. 22401
(703)371-0685

WASHINGTON, D.C.

American Country Antiques
5122 MacArthur Boulevard
Washington, D.C. 20016
(202)363-3628

Mary Emmerling's American Country Store, New York City

Back Country Antiques
2026 R Street N.W.
Washington, D.C. 20009
(202)387-7474

Alan H. Darby
5054 Sherier Place N.W.
Washington, D.C. 20016
(202)244-4822

Design Resources
Elaine Wilmarth
605 Constitution Avenue N.E.
Washington, D.C. 20002
(202)546-6664

The Georgetown Antique Trader
3210 O Street N.W.
Washington, D.C. 20007
(202)333-3004

Marston Luce
1314 21st Street N.W.
Washington, D.C. 20037
(202)775-9460

Nannie's Attic
1511 Wisconsin Avenue N.W.
Georgetown, Washington, D.C. 20007
(202)338-3811

WISCONSIN

American Country Antiques
In the Cedar Creek
Settlement—The Mill
N. 70 W 6340 Bridge Road
Cedarburg, Wis. 53012
(414)375-4140

Willowridge
320 Tower Street
Mineral Point, Wis. 53565
(608)987-3409

June Harrison Antiques, Charlotte, North Carolina

Directory
OF PERIODICALS

The "Directory of Periodicals" lists newspapers, magazines, and journals that are excellent sources of information for collectors. Because there is no central agency providing dates and locations of antiques shows and flea markets, these weekly and monthly antiques periodicals are the best way to find out about events. They also serve as a guide to new dealers and, through ads as well as feature articles, tell where to find and, occasionally, how much to pay for particular pieces.

American Collector
Drawer C
Kermit, Tex. 79745
(915)586-2571

Antique Gazette
929 Davidson Drive
Nashville, Tenn. 37205
(615)352-0941

Antique Monthly
P.O. Box 2274
Birmingham, Alabama 35201
(205)345-0272

The Antique Trader Weekly
P.O. Box 1050
Dubuque, Iowa 52001
(319)588-2073

Antiques & The Arts Weekly
The Bee Publishing Co.
Newtown, Conn. 06470
(203)426-3141

Art & Antiques:
The American Magazine for
Connoisseurs and Collectors
1515 Broadway
New York, N.Y. 10036
(212)764-7300

The Clarion, America's
Folk Art Magazine
Published by:
Museum of American Folk Art
49 West 53rd Street
New York, N.Y. 10019
(212)581-2474

Joel Sater's Antiques &
Auction News
Box B
Marietta, Pa. 17547
(717)426-1956

Kovels on Antiques and
Collectables
P.O. Box 22200
Beachwood, Ohio 44122

The Magazine Antiques
551 Fifth Avenue
New York, N.Y. 10017
(212)922-1818

Maine Antique Digest
Box 3581
Waldoboro, Maine 04572
(207)832-7534

Ohio Antique Review
Box 538
Worthington, Ohio 43085
(614)885-9757

Directory
OF RESTORERS

The "Directory of Restorers" lists experts in the preservation and repair of American Country pieces. Each restorer's area of interest as well as address and phone number is provided. We have included only restorers with an established business, but local antiques dealers can often recommend highly skilled individuals with small practices in the area. Many of the restorers listed on the East Coast have a nationwide clientele.

Ann Anderson
Pa. Star Route, Box 16
Bucks County
Upper Black Eddy, Pa. 18972
(215)294-9441
Specialist in hooked rugs.

Stephen Anderson
New York, N.Y.
(212)431-8354
Specialist in hooked and rag rugs.

Wayne F. Anderson
RFD #1
East Pond Road
Waldoboro, Maine 04572
(207)832-4894
Specialist in fine period furniture in cherry, mahogany, maple, and other finished woods.

Mrs. Badura
New Hope, Pa.
(215)862-2681
Specialist in paintings, not including watercolors.

Bob Barone
195 W. Byers
Denver, Colo. 80223
(303)733-1815
Specialist in quilts.

Susan Butler
Box 134
Turner, Maine 04282
Day: (207)225-3862
Evening: (207)225-2386
Specialist in quilts and hooked rugs.

Cambridge Textiles
Cambridge, N.Y. 12812
Delores Bittleman
Specialist in antique textiles; complete preservation service for fine old quilts and handwoven coverlets. Write for brochure or send article to be restored with details.

Neil and Sue Connell
c/o The Clayton Store
Star Route
Southfield, Mass. 01259
(413)229-2621
By appointment only.
Specialists in painted and decorated furniture, baskets, tins, and bandboxes.

Pie Galiant
New York, N.Y.
(212)832-7077
Specialist in antique quilts; supplies, custom-made stretchers for quilts and hooked rugs; rag carpets sewn together for area rugs.

Harry Holmes
Carter Road and Route 7
Kent, Conn. 06757
(203)297-3420
Specialist in 18th- and 19th-century primitive and fine antique furniture.

Bruce E. Johnson
Iowa City, Iowa
(319)351-2925
Specialist in furniture.

Lew Larason Antiques
Chalfonte, Pa. 18914
(215)822-3987
By appointment only.
Specialist in antique furniture.

David Smith
Morrow, Ohio 45152
(513)932-2472
Specialist in antique furniture.

Textile Conservation Workshop
4225 Russell
Winters, Calif. 95694
(916)795-4605
Specialists in antique quilts and coverlets.

Textile Conservation Workshop
Main Street
South Salem, N.Y. 10590
(914)763-5805
Specialists in antique quilts and coverlets.

Helen Von Rosenstiel
382 11th Street
Brooklyn, N.Y. 11215
(212)788-7909
Specialist in antique rag and hooked rugs, quilts, tapestries, coverlets, samplers, chair covers, and costumes.

The Wood Shaper
Philip Hostetter
181 Christopher Street
New York, N.Y. 10014
(212)255-3051
Specialists in restoration and reproduction of fine furniture.

Index

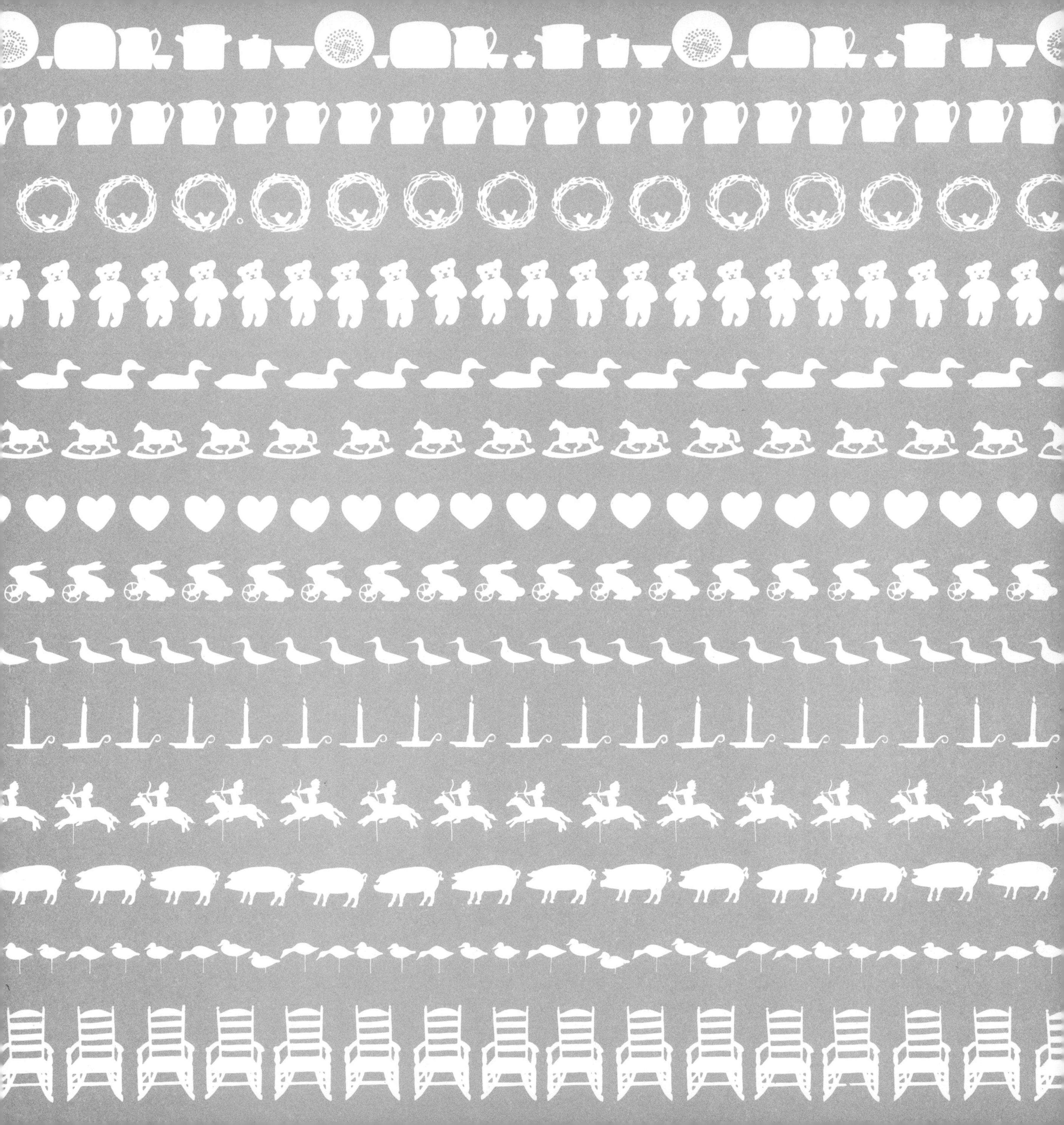

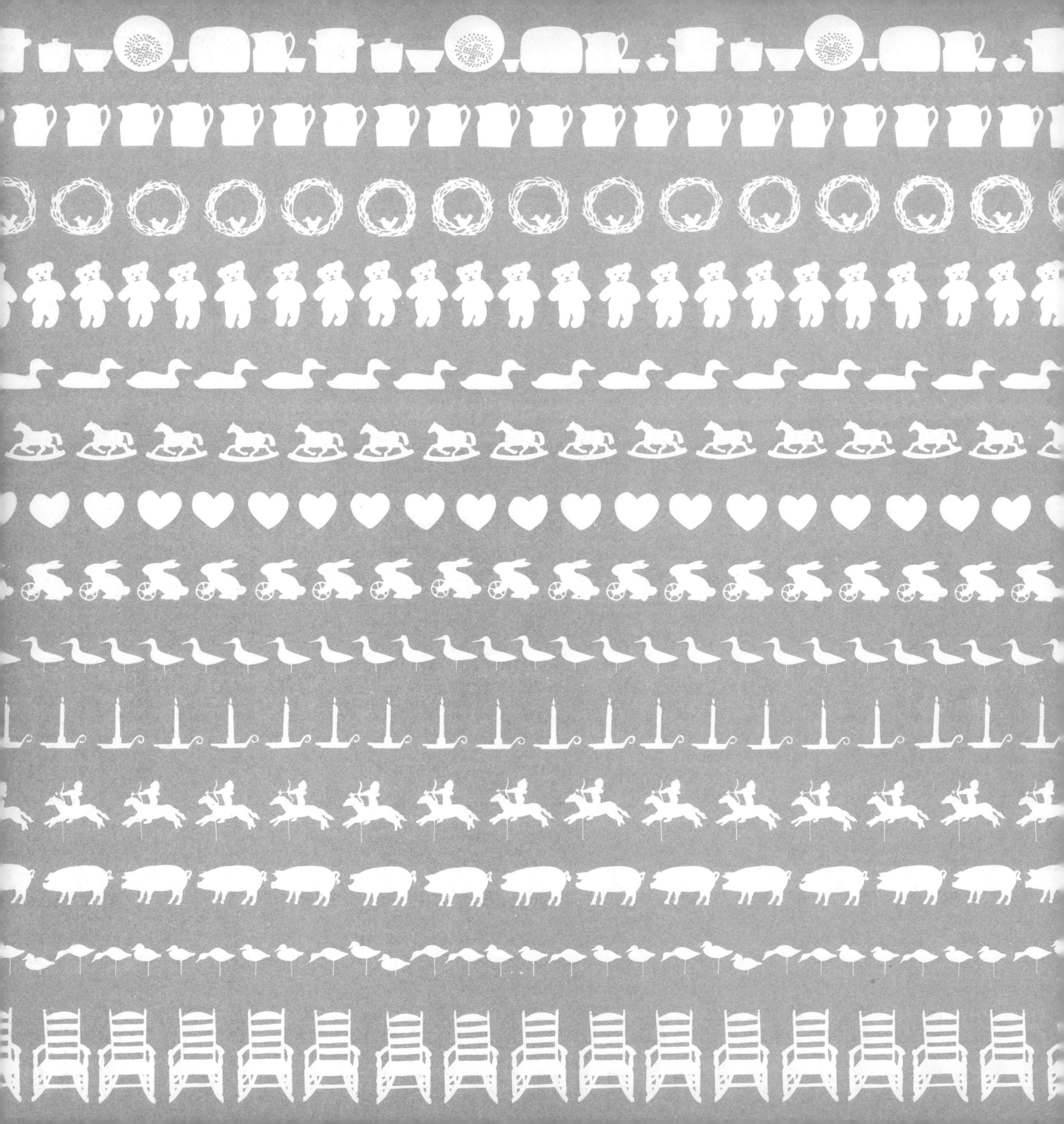